POETRY
OF THE
ZODIAC

DISCOVER THE SECRETS OF EACH SIGN
THROUGH VERSE

POETRY OF THE ZODIAC

EDITED BY LIZ ISON

BATSFORD

CONTENTS

INTRODUCTION

... when I explore the winding courses of the stars
I no longer touch with my feet the Earth:
I am standing near Zeus himself,
drinking my fill of Ambrosia,
the food of the gods.

— Claudius Ptolemy of Alexandria
1st century founder of Western astrology and astronomy
From Anthologia Palatina

The zodiac, rich in metaphors and analogies, with its cyclical and seasonal rhythms, has a deeply poetic core. So exploring astrology through a book of poetry makes perfect sense. Here are poems that burst with the language and imagery of the zodiac, poems that are searching for readers who are fascinated by the wonders of the universe and who wish to embark on a journey of self-discovery and an exploration of the inner life.

Our greatest poets from across the centuries have been inspired not only by nature and the mysteries of the Sun, stars, Moon and heavens, but also by the zodiac, by 'that far-off symbolic writing of the heavens' as writer George Eliot put it. Famously, Shakespeare's plays and poetry are steeped in the vocabulary of the stars. Writers such as 20th century poets W B Yeats and Ted Hughes came to be deeply attracted to astrology in their personal lives as well as finding expression for it in their poetry. Here is poetry that transcends time, place, culture and literary style: Roman writers, medieval philosopher-poets, romantic writers, imagist and contemporary poets. Writers such as Hafiz, Marcus Manilius, Solomon Ibn Gabirol as well as Emily Dickinson, Rilke, Maya Angelou, Elizabeth Jennings and many others bring their versatility and unique perspectives.

Within these pages are poems for each of the 12 star signs, exploring some of the personality traits and outlooks associated with them. Like the art and practice of astrology, the poems can work on a personal level for each reader and I hope this will foster contemplation and curiosity. *Poetry of the Zodiac* aims to open up spaces in which to reflect on how our individual selves interact with the wider world and beyond, and how looking back will help us look forward as well.

While I wouldn't be surprised if you turn to the poems of your own star sign first, I would urge you to take a wander among all of the 12 star signs, each of which come with their own introductory guide. The zodiac, alive with storytelling, myth and the transmission of wisdom, is for everyone; even the sceptic can find stimulation and interest here. Underlying all the signs and the broad personality traits said to be related to them, is a quest for meaning, for love and connection, and an invitation for personal development. This is not so much about destiny as the possibility of transformation. Could the journey to fulfil our potential be found on the turning wheel of the zodiac? Might you find that we are connected with all the facets of the star signs, and that there is unity within its diversity?

A note on the astrology. Each of the signs is named after a constellation, a grouping of stars in the sky, identified and named many centuries ago. One can think of the star signs as telling a sort of narrative both of the cycle of the year, and a story of human life and character. There are ancient myths connected with the constellations and star signs. The characteristics of each star sign are broadly influenced by what are known as the 'elements' and 'modalities' of the zodiac signs as well as their 'polarity' and which planetary body is its associated 'ruler'. These rich layers of meaning have inspired my selection of poetry.

The four elements are fire, earth, air, and water. Each element has qualities and characteristics that it will bring to bear on the star sign so that, for example, fire is creative, earth material, air enlivening and water receptive.

The three modalities are cardinal, fixed, and mutable. These modalities are kinds of modes of operation, so that cardinal could be characterized as having an alpha vibe and is an initiator of change; fixed as focused, stabilizing and unchanging; and mutable as shifting and adaptable.

Each star sign has a polarity, traditionally described as masculine or feminine but may also be called positive or negative, or even yang and yin. Polarities bring contrasting energies to the star signs they are associated with, for example, energetic vs. receptive.

Finally, each star sign has a ruler, that is a planet, the Sun or the Moon associated with it.

The zodiac year begins in March with Aries, the first of the spring signs (for the northern hemisphere) and ends with the last of the winter signs, Pisces. The zodiac's roots in the natural world and the passing seasons act as an earthly counterpoint to the interconnected expanse of the universe which the names of the star signs evoke and so the poetry selected is also often grounded in the beauty and diversity of our natural world.

Let these poems lead you on a journey of self-discovery, and let their words entertain, illuminate, enlighten and dazzle you. In the words of Chilean poet Pablo Neruda, come and wheel through the stars with me, and feel the heavens unfasten.

Liz Ison

ARIES

21 MARCH – 20 APRIL

ARIES

21 MARCH – 20 APRIL

'the wingèd energy of delight'

SYMBOL	RAM
MODALITY	CARDINAL
ELEMENT	FIRE
RULER	MARS
POLARITY	POSITIVE/MASCULINE

ARIES: INTRODUCTION

Aries, symbolized by the Ram, is the first sign of the zodiac and so ushers in new beginnings: dawn, spring, the start of life itself. Not only is Aries the pioneer and leader of the zodiac, but it is also our first fire sign. Aries is ruled by the red planet Mars, who, in mythology, is the god of war.

Those born under this star sign are likely to have strong, independent spirits: to be natural leaders with energy, enthusiasm and spontaneity. With an energetic personality, the typical Aries is bold, competitive and courageous. So arises a direct and determined approach, quick to discern the most important factors in making decisions along with a strong will to succeed.

It feels fitting that the vernal or spring equinox (one of two moments in the yearly cycle when the Sun is exactly above the equator and day and night are of equal length) falls within this astrological sign: after all it is the first cardinal sign of the zodiac and its energy burst awakens the new season, the spring of the northern hemisphere.

Poems for Aries vibrate with the essence of life and sparkle with energy, adventure and a sense of the wonder of our world. Readers whatever their star sign will sense real possibility in these poems: new beginnings, the spark that ignites creativity, change on both a personal and cosmic level and an activated, even explosive, relationship between the individual and the world we live in.

POETRY

And it was at that age ... Poetry arrived
in search of me. I don't know, I don't know where
it came from, from winter or a river.
I don't know how or when,
no, they were not voices, they were not
words, nor silence,
but from a street I was summoned,
from the branches of night,
abruptly from the others,
among violent fires
or returning alone,
there I was without a face
and it touched me.

I did not know what to say, my mouth
had no way
with names,
my eyes were blind,
and something started in my soul,
fever or forgotten wings,
and I made my own way,
deciphering
that fire,
and I wrote the first faint line,
faint, without substance, pure
nonsense,
pure wisdom
of someone who knows nothing,

and suddenly I saw
the heavens
unfastened
and open,
planets,
palpitating plantations,
shadow perforated,
riddled
with arrows, fire and flowers,
the winding night, the universe.

And I, infinitesimal being,
drunk with the great starry
void,
likeness, image of
mystery,
felt myself a pure part
of the abyss,
I wheeled with the stars,
my heart broke loose on the wind.

– Pablo Neruda (1904–1973)
Translated by Alastair Reid

THE WORLD

Extract

I saw Eternity the other night,
Like a great ring of pure and endless light,
All calm, as it was bright;
And round beneath it, Time in hours, days, years,
Driv'n by the spheres
Like a vast shadow mov'd; in which the world
And all her train were hurl'd.

– Henry Vaughan (1621–1695)

AS ONCE THE WINGÈD ENERGY OF DELIGHT

As once the wingèd energy of delight
carried you over childhood's dark abysses,
now beyond your own life build the great
arch of unimagined bridges.

Wonders happen if we can succeed
in passing through the harshest danger;
but only in a bright and purely granted
achievement can we realize the wonder.

To work *with* Things in the indescribable
relationship is not too hard for us;
the pattern grows more intricate and subtle,
and being swept along is not enough.

Take your practiced powers and stretch them out
until they span the chasm between two
contradictions...For the god
wants to know himself in you.

– Rainer Maria Rilke (1875–1926)
Translated by Stephen Mitchell

THE ENKINDLED SPRING

This spring as it comes bursts up in bonfires green,
Wild puffing of green-fire trees, and flame-green bushes,
Thorn-blossom lifting in wreaths of smoke between
Where the wood fumes up and the flickering, watery rushes.

I am amazed at this spring, this conflagration
Of green fires lit on the soil of the earth, this blaze
Of growing, these smoke-puffs that puff in wild gyration,
Faces of people blowing across my gaze!

And I what sort of fire am I among
This conflagration of spring? the gap in it all – !
Not even palish smoke like the rest of the throng,
Less than the wind that runs to the flamy call!

— D H Lawrence (1885–1930)

SONG OF MYSELF

From *Leaves of Grass* (1892)

I celebrate myself, and sing myself,
And what I assume you shall assume,
For every atom belonging to me as good belongs
to you.

I loafe and invite my soul,
I lean and loafe at my ease observing a spear
of summer grass.

My tongue, every atom of my blood, form'd from
this soil, this air,
Born here of parents born here from parents
the same, and their parents the same,
I, now thirty-seven years old in perfect health begin,
Hoping to cease not till death.

Creeds and schools in abeyance,
Retiring back a while sufficed at what they are,
but never forgotten,
I harbor for good or bad, I permit to speak at
every hazard,
Nature without check with original energy.

– Walt Whitman (1819–1892)

THE FOUR ELEMENTS

The Fire, Air, Earth and water did contest
Which was the strongest, noblest and the best,
Who was of greatest use and might'est force;
In placide Terms they thought now to discourse,
That in due order each her turn should speak;
But enmity this amity did break
All would be chief, and all scorn'd to be under
Whence issu'd winds & rains, lightning & thunder
The quaking earth did groan, the Sky lookt black
The Fire, the forced Air, in sunder crack;
The sea did threat the heav'ns, the heavn's the earth,
All looked like a Chaos or new birth:
Fire broyled Earth, & scorched Earth it choaked
Both by their darings, water so provoked
That roaring in it came, and with its source
Soon made the Combatants abate their force
The rumbling hissing, puffing was so great
The worlds confusion, it did seem to threat
Till gentle Air, Contention so abated
That betwixt hot and cold, she arbitrated
The others difference, being less did cease
All storms now laid, and they in perfect peace
That Fire should first begin, the rest consent,
The noblest and most active Element.

— Anne Bradstreet (1612–1672)

HOROSCOPE

You wanted to study
Your stars – the guards
Of your prison yard, their zodiac. The planets
Muttered their Babylonish power-sprach –
Like a witchdoctor's bones. You were right to fear
How loud the bones might roar,
How clear an ear might hear
What the bones whispered
Even embedded as they were in the hot body.

Only you had no need to calculate
Degrees for your ascendant disruptor
In Aries. It meant nothing certain – no more
According to the Babylonian book
Than a scarred face. How much deeper
Under the skin could any magician peep?

You only had to look
Into the nearest face of a metaphor
Picked out of your wardrobe or off your plate
Or out of the sun or the moon or the yew tree
To see your father, your mother, or me
Bringing you your whole Fate.

— Ted Hughes (1930–1998)

THE YEAR'S AWAKENING

How do you know that the pilgrim track
Along the belting zodiac
Swept by the sun in his seeming rounds
Is traced by now to the Fishes' bounds
And into the Ram, when weeks of cloud
Have wrapt the sky in a clammy shroud,
And never as yet a tinct of spring
Has shown in the Earth's apparelling;
   O vespering bird, how do you know,
      How do you know?

How do you know, deep underground,
Hid in your bed from sight and sound,
Without a turn in temperature,
With weather life can scarce endure,
That light has won a fraction's strength,
And day put on some moments' length,
Whereof in merest rote will come,
Weeks hence, mild airs that do not numb;
   O crocus root, how do you know,
      How do you know?

— Thomas Hardy (1840–1928)

HEAVEN AND EARTH

I survey the heavens and the stars;
I look at the earth with its creeping creatures;
and I understand in my heart that they were all
intricately fashioned.
Look up at the sky – like a tent, whose clasps are joined
to it by loops;
the moon and its stars – like a shepherdess grazing her
flock in a pasture;
the moon among the sweeping clouds – like a ship sailing
with raised pennants;
a cloud – like a girl walking through a garden, watering
the myrtles;
a cloud of dew – like a maiden shaking the drops from her
hair onto the ground.
But the earth's inhabitants are like an army
pitching its tents for a night, looting the local granaries.
And all flee before the terror of death – like a dove chased
by a hawk.
All are doomed to be like an earthenware plate which has
been smashed to bits.

— Samuel Hanagid (c. 993–1056)
Translated by T Carmi

TAURUS
21 APRIL – 21 MAY

TAURUS

21 APRIL – 21 MAY

'touching the surface and the depths of things'

SYMBOL	BULL
MODALITY	FIXED
ELEMENT	EARTH
RULER	VENUS
POLARITY	NEGATIVE/FEMININE

TAURUS: INTRODUCTION

After the zodiac's wonderfully energetic and creative start in Aries, Taurus's vibe is abundantly earthy: it is the star sign of our world when it turns green in spring. Where Aries created, Taurus gives it form and substance. It is time to enjoy and savour the pleasures and beauty of the planet.

Taurus is the first of the three earth signs and is ruled by the planet Venus, which is said to add a sensual side. Symbolized by the bull (the 'Bull of Heaven' being one of the most ancient of Babylonian symbols of fertility and power), Taurus is also a fixed sign which brings a quality of focus, firmness and persistence.

People born under this star sign tend to be warm-hearted, reliable and loyal. Their dependable nature makes them willing to take on responsibility. Although they can be tenacious and steadfast, they are firmly grounded in reality which can make them slow and cautious at times. Fantastically attuned to the world, and to their place in it, they are also romantic, kind and gentle. They are responsive to all that is beautiful. They will take great joy in making people happy and ensuring that everyone feels at ease.

Poems for Taurus communicate abundance and they are of the earth: grounded and strong; not ethereal, but of real substance and deep-rooted. These are poems of celebration: celebrating the world, our earthly home, the universe and our own unique place in it: to be enjoyed, to be experienced, in which to be alive.

NOW TURNING FROM THE WINTRY SIGNS

From *The Flower And The Leaf; or, the Lady In The Arbour. A Vision*

Now turning from the wintry Signs, the Sun
His Course exalted through the Ram had run:
And whirling up the Skies, his Chariot drove
Through *Taurus*, and the lightsome Realms of Love,
Where *Venus* from her Orb descends in Show'rs
To glad the Ground, and paint the Fields with Flow'rs:
When first the tender Blades of Grass appear,
And Buds, that yet the blast of *Eurus* fear,
Stand at the door of Life, and doubt to clothe the Year;
Till gentle Heat, and soft repeated Rains,
Make the green Blood to dance within their Veins:
Then, at their Call embolden'd out they come,
And swell the Gems, and burst the narrow Room;
Broader and broader yet, their Blooms display,
Salute the welcome Sun, and entertain the Day.
Then from their breathing Souls the Sweets repair
To scent the Skies, and purge th' unwholesome Air:
Joy spreads the Heart, and with a general Song,
Spring issues out, and leads the jolly Months along.

– John Dryden (1631–1700)

TO BE OF USE

The people I love the best
jump into work head first
without dallying in the shallows
and swim off with sure strokes almost out of sight.
They seem to become natives of that element,
the black sleek heads of seals
bouncing like half-submerged balls.

I love people who harness themselves, an ox to a heavy cart,
who pull like water buffalo, with massive patience,
who strain in the mud and the muck to move things forward,
who do what has to be done, again and again.

I want to be with people who submerge
in the task, who go into the fields to harvest
and work in a row and pass the bags along,
who are not parlor generals and field deserters
but move in a common rhythm
when the food must come in or the fire be put out.

The work of the world is common as mud.
Botched, it smears the hands, crumbles to dust.
But the thing worth doing well done
has a shape that satisfies, clean and evident.
Greek amphoras for wine or oil,
Hopi vases that held corn, are put in museums
but you know they were made to be used.
The pitcher cries for water to carry
and a person for work that is real.

– Marge Piercy (b. 1936)

LIKE A STRONG TREE

Like a strong tree that in the virgin earth
Sends far its roots through rock and loam and clay,
And proudly thrives in rain or time of dearth,
When the dry waves scare rainy sprites away;
Like a strong tree that reaches down, deep, deep,
For sunken water, fluid underground,
Where the great-ringed unsightly blind worms creep,
And queer things of the nether world abound:

So would I live in rich imperial growth,
Touching the surface and the depth of things,
Instinctively responsive unto both,
Tasting the sweets of being and the stings,
Sensing the subtle spell of changing forms,
Like a strong tree against a thousand storms.

— Claude McKay (1889–1948)

IN MY CRAFT OR SULLEN ART

In my craft or sullen art
Exercised in the still night
When only the moon rages
And the lovers lie abed
With all their griefs in their arms,
I labour by singing light
Not for ambition or bread
Or the strut and trade of charms
On the ivory stages
But for the common wages
Of their most secret heart.

Not for the proud man apart
From the raging moon I write
On these spindrift pages
Nor for the towering dead
With their nightingales and psalms
But for the lovers, their arms
Round the griefs of the ages,
Who pay no praise or wages
Nor heed my craft or art.

– Dylan Thomas (1914–1953)

'... WHERE ARE YOU HURRYING TO?'

From *The Epic of Gilgamesh*
Following Gilgamesh's battle with the Bull of Heaven

'... where are you hurrying to?
You will never find that life for which you are looking.
...fill your belly with good things;
day and night, night and day,
dance and be merry, feast and rejoice.
Let your clothes be fresh, bathe yourself in water,
cherish the little child that holds your hand,
and make your wife happy in your embrace;
for this too is the lot of man.'

– Anon of Babylon (written c. 2100–1200 BCE)
Translated by N K Sandars

EACH MOMENT A WHITE BULL STEPS SHINING INTO THE WORLD

If the gods bring to you
a strange and frightening creature,
accept the gift
as if it were one you had chosen.

Say the accustomed prayers,
oil the hooves well,
caress the small ears with praise.

Have the new halter of woven silver
embedded with jewels.
Spare no expense, pay what is asked,
when a gift arrives from the sea.

Treat it as you yourself
would be treated,
brought speechless and naked
into the court of a king.

And when the request finally comes,
do not hesitate even an instant –

Stroke the white throat,
the heavy, trembling dewlaps
you've come to believe were yours,
and plunge in the knife.

Not once
did you enter the pasture
without pause,
without yourself trembling.
That you came to love it, that was the gift.

Let the envious gods take back what they can.

— Jane Hirshfield (b. 1953)

THE THINGS DIVINE

These are the things I hold divine:
A trusting child's hand laid in mine,
Rich brown earth and wind-tossed trees,
The taste of grapes and the drone of bees,
A rhythmic gallop, long June days,
A rose-hedged lane and lovers' lays,
The welcome smile on neighbors' faces,
Cool, wide hills and open places,
Breeze-blown fields of silver rye,
The wild, sweet note of the plover's cry,
Fresh spring showers and scent of box,
The soft, pale tint of the garden phlox,
Lilacs blooming, a drowsy noon,
A flight of geese and an autumn moon,
Rolling meadows and storm-washed heights,
A fountain murmur on summer nights,
A dappled fawn in the forest hush,
Simple words and the song of a thrush,
Rose-red dawns and a mate to share
With comrade soul my gypsy fare,
A waiting fire when the twilight ends,
A gallant heart and the voice of friends.

– Jean Brooks Burt (dates unknown)

SONG OF NATURE

Verses 1–9

Mine are the night and morning,
The pits of air, the gulf of space,
The sportive sun, the gibbous moon,
The innumerable days.

I hide in the solar glory,
I am dumb in the pealing song,
I rest on the pitch of the torrent,
In slumber I am strong.

No numbers have counted my tallies,
No tribes my house can fill,
I sit by the shining Fount of Life,
And pour the deluge still;

And ever by delicate powers
Gathering along the centuries
From race on race the rarest flowers,
My wreath shall nothing miss.

And many a thousand summers
My apples ripened well,
And light from meliorating stars
With firmer glory fell.

I wrote the past in characters
Of rock and fire the scroll,
The building in the coral sea,
The planting of the coal.

And thefts from satellites and rings
And broken stars I drew,
And out of spent and aged things
I formed the world anew;

What time the gods kept carnival,
Tricked out in star and flower,
And in cramp elf and saurian forms
They swathed their too much power.

Time and Thought were my surveyors,
They laid their courses well,
They boiled the sea, and baked the layers
Of granite, marl and shell.

— Ralph Waldo Emerson (1803–1882)

THE GARDEN

Extract

What wondrous life is this I lead!
Ripe apples drop about my head;
The luscious clusters of the vine
Upon my mouth do crush their wine;
The nectarine, and curious peach
Into my hands themselves do reach;
Stumbling on melons as I pass,
Insnared with flowers, I fall on grass.

Meanwhile the mind, from pleasure less,
Withdraws into its happiness;
The mind, that ocean where each kind
Does straight its own resemblance find;
Yet it creates, transcending these,
Far other worlds, and other seas;
Annihilating all that's made
To a green thought in a green shade.

...

How well the skillful gardener drew
Of flowers and herbs this dial new,
Where from above the milder sun
Does through a fragrant zodiac run,
And as it works, the industrious bee
Computes its time as well as we!
How could such sweet and wholesome hours
Be reckoned but with herbs and flowers?

– Andrew Marvell (1621–1678)

THOUGH DUSTY WITS SCORN ASTROLOGY

Though dusty wits dare scorn astrology,
And fools can think those lamps of purest light
Whose numbers weigh greatness, eternity,
Promising wonders, wonder do invite,
To have, for no cause, birthright in the sky,
But for to spangle the black weeds of night:
Or for some brawl, which in that chamber high,
They should still dance to please a gazer's sight.

For me, I do nature unidle know,
And know great causes, great effects procure;
And know, those bodies high reign on the low.
And if these rules did fail, proof makes me sure,
Who oft fore-judge my after-following race,
By only those two stars in Stella's face.

– Sir Philip Sidney (1554–1586)

GEMINI
22 MAY – 21 JUNE

GEMINI

22 MAY – 21 JUNE

'truth was to me a breath, a wind, a shadow'

SYMBOL	TWINS
MODALITY	MUTABLE
ELEMENT	AIR
RULER	MERCURY
POLARITY	POSITIVE/MASCULINE

GEMINI: INTRODUCTION

Gemini is a mutable, masculine air sign. Gemini takes its name from the twin stars in this portion of the sky (in Latin 'gemini' means twins). The twins are said to be the half-brothers of Greek and Roman mythology, Castor and Pollux.

The duality of the star sign suggests that a goal of Geminis should be to unite the opposites within them, and to come to a unified understanding of the human condition and its limitations. The mutable nature of the sign means that Geminis can be restless and volatile, but also flexible, quick and inquisitive. This versatility allows them to pursue several paths of action at once, and take note of different perspectives.

Ruled by the planet Mercury (named for the messenger of the gods), Geminis are eloquent, communicative, sociable and witty, with a love of learning. This is a star sign of the intellect: curious, with wide-ranging knowledge of life, excited by everything the world has to offer.

Poems for Gemini have breadth, with a sweeping scope. As the star sign of language, these poems are full of invention and a quest for truth even when truth can often feel elusive. Readers will nonetheless notice their minds expand by the questioning and shifting voices in search of meaning. Given the sign's air element, these living, breathing Gemini poems will make us all feel more alive.

WILD AIR, WORLD-MOTHERING AIR

From *The Blessed Virgin compared to the Air we Breathe*

Wild air, world-mothering air,
Nestling me everywhere,
That each eyelash or hair
Girdles; goes home betwixt
The fleeciest, frailest-flixed
Snowflake; that's fairly mixed
With, riddles, and is rife
In every least thing's life;
This needful, never spent,
And nursing element;
My more than meat and drink,
My meal at every wink;
This air, which, by life's law,
My lung must draw and draw
Now but to breathe its praise

– Gerard Manley Hopkins (1844–1889)

I STOOD UPON A STAR

I stretched my mind until I stood
  Out in space, upon a star;
I looked, and saw the flying earth
  Where seven planets are.

Delicately interweaving
  Like fireflies on a moist June night,
The planetoids among the planets
  Played for their own delight

I watched earth putting off her winter
  And slipping into green;
I saw the dark side of the moon
  No man has ever seen.

Like shining wheels in an opened watch
  They all revolved with soundless motion;
Each sparkled like a rain-wet flower,
  Bearing petals, plain and ocean.

— *Sara Teasdale (1884–1933)*

'TRUTH,' SAID A TRAVELLER

'Truth,' said a traveller,
'Is a rock, a mighty fortress;
'Often have I been to it,
'Even to its highest tower,
'From whence the world looks black.'

'Truth,' said a traveller,
'Is a breath, a wind,
'A shadow, a phantom;
'Long have I pursued it,
'But never have I touched
'The hem of its garment.'

And I believed the second traveller;
For truth was to me
A breath, a wind,
A shadow, a phantom,
And never had I touched
The hem of its garment.

— Stephen Crane (1871–1900)

THE MYSTERY OF PRESENCE

The mystery of presence
will not arrive through the mind,
but do some physical work, and it comes clear.

An intellectual gets bound and wrapped
in complicated nets of connectedness.
Whereas the Friend rides the intelligence
that is creating genius at the center.

The mind is husk, and the appetites love coverings.
They look for them everywhere.
That which loves the kernel and the oil
inside the nut has no interest in shells.

Mind carries reams of reasons into court,
but universal awareness does not move a step
without some definite intuition.
One covers volumes of pages.
The other fills the horizon with light and color.

The value of scrip resides in gold
stored somewhere else. The value of a body
stems from the soul. The value of soul
derives from presence. Soul cannot live
without a connection there.

— Rumi (1207–1273)
Translated by Coleman Barks

YE STARS! WHICH ARE THE POETRY OF HEAVEN

From *Childe Harold's Pilgrimage* Canto III

Ye stars! which are the poetry of heaven!
If in your bright leaves we would read the fate
Of men and empires, – 'tis to be forgiven,
That in our aspirations to be great,
Our destinies o'erleap their mortal state,
And claim a kindred with you; for ye are
A beauty and a mystery, and create
In us such love and reverence from afar,
That fortune, fame, power, life, have named themselves a star.

— Lord Byron (1788–1824)

A FIRST CONFESSION

I admit the briar
Entangled in my hair
Did not injure me;
My blenching and trembling
Nothing but dissembling,
Nothing but coquetry.

I long for truth, and yet
I cannot stay from that
My better self disowns,
For a man's attention
Brings such satisfaction
To the craving in my bones.

Brightness that I pull back
From the Zodiac,
Why those questioning eyes
That are fixed upon me?
What can they do but shun me
If empty night replies?

— W B Yeats (1865–1939)

IN SPITE OF EVERYTHING, THE STARS

Like a stunned piano, like a bucket
of fresh milk flung into the air
or a dozen fists of confetti
thrown hard at a bride
stepping down from the altar,
the stars surprise the sky.
Think of dazed stones
floating overhead, or an ocean
of starfish hung up to dry. Yes,
like a conductor's expectant arm
about to lift toward the chorus,
or a juggler's plates defying gravity,
or a hundred fastballs fired at once
and freezing in midair, the stars
startle the sky over the city.

And that's why drunks leaning up
against abandoned buildings, women
hurrying home on deserted side streets,
policemen turning blind corners, and
even thieves stepping from alleys
all stare up at once. Why else do
sleepwalkers move toward the windows,
or old men drag flimsy lawn chairs
onto fire escapes, or hardened criminals
press sad foreheads to steel bars?
Because the night is alive with lamps!
That's why in dark houses all over the city
dreams stir in the pillows, a million
plumes of breath rise into the sky.

– Edward Hirsch (b. 1950)

A SONG OF OPPOSITES

Welcome joy, and welcome sorrow,
  Lethe's weed and Hermes' feather;
Come today, and come tomorrow,
  I do love you both together!
  I love to mark sad faces in fair weather;
And hear a merry laugh amid the thunder;
  Fair and foul I love together.
Meadows sweet where flames are under,
And a giggle at a wonder;
Visage sage at pantomime;
Funeral, and steeple-chime;
Infant playing with a skull;
Morning fair, and shipwreck'd hull;
Nightshade with the woodbine kissing;
Serpents in red roses hissing;
Cleopatra regal-dress'd
With the aspic at her breast;
Dancing music, music sad,
Both together, sane and mad;
Muses bright and muses pale;
Sombre Saturn, Momus hale; –
Laugh and sigh, and laugh again;
Oh the sweetness of the pain!
Muses bright, and muses pale,
Bare your faces of the veil;
Let me see; and let me write
Of the day, and of the night –
Both together: – let me slake

All my thirst for sweet heart-ache!
Let my bower be of yew,
Interwreath'd with myrtles new;
Pines and lime-trees full in bloom,
And my couch a low grass-tomb.

– John Keats (1795–1821)

NOT FROM THE STARS DO I MY JUDGMENT PLUCK

Sonnet 14

Not from the stars do I my judgment pluck,
And yet methinks I have astronomy –
But not to tell of good or evil luck,
Of plagues, of dearths, or seasons' quality;
Nor can I fortune to brief minutes tell,
Pointing to each his thunder, rain, and wind,
Or say with princes if it shall go well
By oft predict that I in heaven find.
But from thine eyes my knowledge I derive,
And, constant stars, in them I read such art
As truth and beauty shall together thrive
If from thyself to store thou wouldst convert;
 Or else of thee this I prognosticate:
 Thy end is truth's and beauty's doom and date.

— William Shakespeare (1564–1616)

SONG OF THE SPRING TO THE SUMMER

The poet sings to her poet

O poet of the time to be,
My conqueror, I began for thee.
  Enter into thy poet's pain,
  And take the riches of the rain,
And make the perfect year for me.

Thou unto whom my lyre shall fall,
Whene'er thou comest, hear my call.
  O, keep the promise of my lays,
  Take the sweet parable of my days;
I trust thee with the aim of all.

And if thy thoughts unfold from me,
Know that I too have hints of thee,
  Dim hopes that come across my mind
  In the rare days of warmer wind,
And tones of summer in the sea.

And I have set thy paths, I guide
Thy blossoms on the wild hillside.
  And I, thy bygone poet, share
  The flowers that throng thy feet where'er
I led thy feet before I died.

– Alice Meynell (1847–1922)

CANCER
22 JUNE – 22 JULY

CANCER

22 JUNE – 22 JULY

'I shall take my scattered selves and make them one'

SYMBOL	CRAB
MODALITY	CARDINAL
ELEMENT	WATER
RULER	MOON
POLARITY	NEGATIVE/FEMININE

CANCER: INTRODUCTION

Like other star signs that share a cardinal – or primary – element, Cancer heralds the beginning of a new season. While Aries ushered in spring with its fiery element, Cancer – the first of the water signs – is our gateway to summer.

Cancer is uniquely ruled by the Moon (every other sign is ruled by a planet or, in the case of Leo, the Sun).

Cancer's symbol of the crab is derived from the ancient Greek story of the legendary hero Heracles who was pinched by a crab while he was in combat with a terrifying serpentine lake monster (the Lernaean hydra). Heracles managed to crush the crab, but his enemy and persecutor, Hera (wife of Zeus), rewarded the crab by placing him in the heavens, to become immortalized as a constellation.

Nurturing and compassionate, those born under this star sign are incredibly in touch with the world around them. They can connect with the wisdom of the earth, to the point, it seems, of having psychic intuition. Imagination combined with this depth of emotion makes them likely to be loving, sympathetic, kind, intuitive and family-oriented, but also enigmatic, tenacious and protective but prone to worry.

Poems for Cancer tap into the zodiacal zeitgeist and come with a luminous lunar aura. There is an openness and expansiveness to this selection, which means the poetry can feel at times like a listening, soft but strong presence. There is a deep and nurturing thoughtfulness here as well as a touch of nostalgia which may make readers slow down, ponder and re-read.

INTERLUDES

Not a beginning, not an end,
this neutral place
is rich with stillness,
with movement in all directions.
In the words of the prophet, we
are travellers. So pass in peace, stranger,
though our orbits differ,
I too have rested here at these
limbo interludes
in our shared planet's rotation.
So catch your breath and let my words
welcome you like a friend's blessing.
May this space around you expand
and glow in the warmth of knowing
that it's only a corridor;
not a beginning, not an end,
but a green oasis.

– Debjani Chatterjee (b. 1952)

TO A CHILD

Extract

By what astrology of fear or hope
Dare I to cast thy horoscope!
Like the new moon thy life appears;
A little strip of silver light,
And widening outward into night
The shadowy disk of future years;
And yet upon its outer rim,
A luminous circle, faint and dim,
And scarcely visible to us here,
Rounds and completes the perfect sphere;
A prophecy and intimation,
A pale and feeble adumbration,
Of the great world of light, that lies
Behind all human destinies.

...

Enough! I will not play the Seer;
I will no longer strive to ope
The mystic volume, where appear
The herald Hope, forerunning Fear,
And Fear, the pursuivant of Hope.
Thy destiny remains untold;
For, like Acestes' shaft of old,
The swift thought kindles as it flies,
And burns to ashes in the skies.

– Henry Wadsworth Longfellow (1807–1882)

FERN HILL

Now as I was young and easy under the apple boughs
About the lilting house and happy as the grass was green,
The night above the dingle starry,
Time let me hail and climb
Golden in the heydays of his eyes,
And honoured among wagons I was prince of the apple towns
And once below a time I lordly had the trees and leaves
Trail with daisies and barley
Down the rivers of the windfall light.

And as I was green and carefree, famous among the barns
About the happy yard and singing as the farm was home,
In the sun that is young once only,
Time let me play and be
Golden in the mercy of his means,
And green and golden I was huntsman and herdsman, the calves
Sang to my horn, the foxes on the hills barked clear and cold,
And the sabbath rang slowly
In the pebbles of the holy streams.

All the sun long it was running, it was lovely, the hay
Fields high as the house, the tunes from the chimneys, it was air
And playing, lovely and watery
And fire green as grass.
And nightly under the simple stars
As I rode to sleep the owls were bearing the farm away,
All the moon long I heard, blessed among stables, the nightjars
Flying with the ricks, and the horses
Flashing into the dark.

And then to awake, and the farm, like a wanderer white
With the dew, come back, the cock on his shoulder: it was all
  Shining, it was Adam and maiden,
    The sky gathered again
  And the sun grew round that very day.
So it must have been after the birth of the simple light
In the first, spinning place, the spellbound horses walking warm
  Out of the whinnying green stable
    On to the fields of praise.

And honoured among foxes and pheasants by the gay house
Under the new made clouds and happy as the heart was long,
  In the sun born over and over,
    I ran my heedless ways,
  My wishes raced through the house high hay
And nothing I cared, at my sky blue trades, that time allows
In all his tuneful turning so few and such morning songs
  Before the children green and golden
    Follow him out of grace,

Nothing I cared, in the lamb white days, that time would take me
Up to the swallow thronged loft by the shadow of my hand,
  In the moon that is always rising,
    Nor that riding to sleep
  I should hear him fly with the high fields
And wake to the farm forever fled from the childless land.
Oh as I was young and easy in the mercy of his means,
    Time held me green and dying
  Though I sang in my chains like the sea.

— Dylan Thomas (1914–1953)

THE CRYSTAL GAZER

I shall gather myself into myself again,
   I shall take my scattered selves and make them one,
Fusing them into a polished crystal ball
   Where I can see the moon and the flashing sun.

I shall sit like a sibyl, hour after hour intent,
   Watching the future come and the present go,
And the little shifting pictures of people rushing
   In restless self-importance to and fro.

– Sara Teasdale (1884–1933)

STARS AND PLANETS

Trees are cages for them: water holds its breath
To balance them without smudging on its delicate meniscus.
Children watch them playing in their heavenly playground;
Men use them to lug ships across oceans, through firths.

They seem so twinkle-still, but they never cease
Inventing new spaces and huge explosions
And migrating in mathematical tribes over
The steppes of space at their outrageous ease.

It's hard to think that the earth is one –
This poor sad bearer of wars and disasters
Rolls-Roycing round the sun with its load of gangsters,
Attended only by the loveless moon.

— Norman MacCaig (1910–1996)

LADY LUNA, IN LIGHT CANOE

From *The Planets*

Lady LUNA, in light canoe,
By friths and shallows of fretted cloudland
Cruises monthly; with chrism of dews
And drench of dream, a drizzling glamour,
Enchants us – the cheat! changing sometime
A mind to madness, melancholy pale,
Bleached with gazing on her blank count'nance
Orb'd and ageless. In earth's bosom
The shower of her rays, sharp-feathered light
Reaching downward, ripens silver,
Forming and fashioning female brightness,
– Metal maidenlike. Her moist circle
Is nearest earth.

— C S Lewis (1898–1963)

THE PRESENT

For the present there is just one moon,
though every level pond gives back another.

But the bright disc shining in the black lagoon,
perceived by astrophysicist and lover,

is milliseconds old. And even that light's
seven minutes older than its source.

And the stars we think we see on moonless nights
are long extinguished. And, of course,

this very moment, as you read this line,
is literally gone before you know it.

Forget the here-and-now. We have no time
but this device of wantonness and wit.

Make me this present then: your hand in mine,
and we'll live out our lives in it.

— Michael Donaghy (1954–2004)

FLOATING ON THE POOL OF JO YA SPRING

Solitary meditation is not suddenly snapped off; it continues
without interruption.
It flows – drifts this way, that way – returns upon itself.
The boat moves before a twilight wind.
We enter the mouth of the pool by the flower path
At the moment when night enfolds the Western Valley.
The serrated hills face the Southern Constellation,
Mist hangs over the deep river pools and floats down gently,
gently, with the current.
Behind me, through the trees, the moon is sinking.
The business of the world is a swiftly moving space of water,
a rushing, spreading water.
I am content to be an old man holding a bamboo fishing-rod.

– Chi Wu-Ch'ien (c. 733)
Translated by Florence Ayscough and Amy Lowell

I WISH I COULD SHOW YOU

I wish I could show you,
When you are lonely or in darkness,
The Astonishing Light
of your own Being!

— Hafiz (1310–1390)
Translated by Daniel Ladinsky

LEO

23 JULY – 22 AUGUST

LEO

23 JULY – 22 AUGUST

'Rise like Lions'

SYMBOL	LION
MODALITY	FIXED
ELEMENT	FIRE
RULER	SUN
POLARITY	POSITIVE/MASCULINE

LEO: INTRODUCTION

Leo is a fixed, masculine fire sign and is unique as it is ruled by the Sun. It is the sign of self-expression: confident, charismatic and loving to be the centre of attention. Leo is symbolized as a lion with its origins in the story of the mythical Nemean lion slain by Heracles.

So many strong positive qualities are associated with this star sign: generosity, enthusiasm, faithfulness and sociability are just some of them. Those with this star sign often have a powerful creative urge that must be expressed otherwise there is a risk of wasted potential. But this expansive mindset – warmed by the Sun – must be tempered to avoid becoming overbearing or demanding. Often popular, they draw people to them by their audacious energy and spontaneous approach to life.

Poems for Leo exude confidence and will energize readers with their zest for life, adventurous spirit and the sinewy strength embodied in their verses. Such enthusiasm, steadfastness and surety of self will surely rub off and encourage all of us – whether Leos or not – to embrace a sunny optimism and express our inner roar.

DON'T FLEE FROM HARDSHIPS

***Aeneid* 6, 95**

Don't flee from hardships
but meet them more bravely
than your fate would allow

— *Virgil (70 BCE–19 BCE)*

SOLAR

Suspended lion face
Spilling at the centre
Of an unfurnished sky
How still you stand,
And how unaided
Single stalkless flower
You pour unrecompensed.

The eye sees you
Simplified by distance
Into an origin,
Your petalled head of flames
Continuously exploding.
Heat is the echo of your
Gold.

Coined there among
Lonely horizontals
You exist openly.
Our needs hourly
Climb and return like angels.
Unclosing like a hand,
You give for ever.

– Philip Larkin (1922–1985)

VARIATION ON A THEME BY RILKE

A certain day became a presence to me;
there it was, confronting me – a sky, air, light:
a being. And before it started to descend
from the height of noon, it leaned over
and struck my shoulder as if with
the flat of a sword, granting me
honor and a task. The day's blow
rang out, metallic – or it was I, a bell awakened,
and what I heard was my whole self
saying and singing what it knew: *I can*.

— Denise Levertov (1923–1997)

WILL

There is no chance, no destiny, no fate,
  Can circumvent or hinder or control
  The firm resolve of a determined soul.
Gifts count for nothing; will alone is great;
All things give way before it, soon or late.
  What obstacle can stay the mighty force
  Of the sea-seeking river in its course,
Or cause the ascending orb of day to wait?
Each well-born soul must win what it deserves.
Let the fool prate of luck. The fortunate
  Is he whose earnest purpose never swerves,
  Whose slightest action or inaction serves
The one great aim.
              Why, even Death stands still,
And waits an hour sometimes for such a will.

— Ella Wheeler Wilcox (1850–1919)

POEM OF THE ROAD

Extract

Afoot and light-hearted I take to the open road,
Healthy, free, the world before me,
The long brown path before me, leading wherever I choose.

Henceforth I ask not good-fortune – I myself am good-fortune;
Henceforth I whimper no more, postpone no more, need nothing,
Strong and content, I travel the open road.

The earth – that is sufficient,
I do not want the constellations any nearer,
I know they are very well where they are,
I know they suffice for those who belong to them.

...

I inhale great draughts of air,
The east and the west are mine, and the north and the south
are mine.

— *Walt Whitman (1819–1892)*

THE MASQUE OF ANARCHY

Verses 90–91

'And these words shall then become
Like Oppression's thundered doom
Ringing through each heart and brain,
Heard again - again - again -

'Rise like Lions after slumber
In unvanquishable number -
Shake your chains to earth like dew
Which in sleep had fallen on you -
Ye are many - they are few.'

— *Percy Bysshe Shelley (1792–1822)*

SET ME WHERE AS THE SUN DOTH PARCH THE GREEN

Set me where as the sun doth parch the green,
Or where his beams do not dissolve the ice;
In temperate heat where he is felt and seen;
With proud people, in presence sad and wise;
Set me in base, or yet in high degree,
In the long night, or in the shortest day,
In clear weather, or where mists thickest be,
In lost youth, or when my hairs be grey;
Set me in earth, in heaven, or yet in hell,
In hill, in dale, or in the foaming flood;
Thrall, or at large, alive where so I dwell,
Sick, or in health, in ill fame or good:
Yours will I be, and with that only thought
Comfort myself when that my hope is nought.

– Henry Howard (1517–1547)

SONGS FOR THE PEOPLE

Let me make the songs for the people,
  Songs for the old and young;
Songs to stir like a battle-cry
  Wherever they are sung.

Not for the clashing of sabres,
  For carnage nor for strife;
But songs to thrill the hearts of men
  With more abundant life.

Let me make the songs for the weary,
  Amid life's fever and fret,
Till hearts shall relax their tension,
  And careworn brows forget.

Let me sing for little children,
  Before their footsteps stray,
Sweet anthems of love and duty,
  To float o'er life's highway.

I would sing for the poor and aged,
  When shadows dim their sight;
Of the bright and restful mansions,
  Where there shall be no night.

Our world, so worn and weary,
  Needs music, pure and strong,
To hush the jangle and discords
  Of sorrow, pain, and wrong.

Music to soothe all its sorrow,
   Till war and crime shall cease;
And the hearts of men grown tender
   Girdle the world with peace.

– Frances Ellen Watkins Harper (1825–1911)

ULYSSES

Extract

The long day wanes: the slow moon climbs: the deep
Moans round with many voices. Come, my friends,
'Tis not too late to seek a newer world.
Push off, and sitting well in order smite
The sounding furrows; for my purpose holds
To sail beyond the sunset, and the baths
Of all the western stars, until I die.
It may be that the gulfs will wash us down:
It may be we shall touch the Happy Isles,
And see the great Achilles, whom we knew.
Tho' much is taken, much abides; and tho'
We are not now that strength which in old days
Moved earth and heaven, that which we are, we are;
One equal temper of heroic hearts,
Made weak by time and fate, but strong in will
To strive, to seek, to find, and not to yield.

— Alfred, Lord Tennyson (1809–1892)

LET THERE BE LIGHTS

From *Paradise Lost* Book VII

... Let there be Lights
High in the expanse of Heaven, to divide
The day from night: and let them be for signs,
For seasons, and for days, and circling years;
And let them be for lights, as I ordain
Their office in the firmament of Heaven,
To give light on the earth; and it was so.
And God made two great lights, great for their use
To Man, the greater to have rule by day,
The less by night, altern; and made the stars,
And set them in the firmament of Heaven
To illuminate the earth, and rule the day
In their vicissitude, and rule the night,
And light from darkness to divide. God saw,
Surveying his great work, that it was good:
For, of celestial bodies, first the sun
A mighty sphere, he framed, unlightsome first,
Though of ethereal mould: then formed the moon
Globose, and every magnitude of stars,
And sowed with stars the Heaven, thick as a field:
Of light by far the greater part he took,
Transplanted from her cloudy shrine, and placed
In the sun's orb, made porous to receive
And drink the liquid light; firm to retain
Her gathered beams, great palace now of light.
Hither, as to their fountain, other stars

Repairing, in their golden urns draw light,
And hence the morning planet gilds her horns;
By tincture or reflection they augment
Their small peculiar, though for human sight
So far remote, with diminution seen,
First in his east the glorious lamp was seen,
Regent of day, and all the horizon round
Invested with bright rays jocund to run
His longitude through Heaven's high road. The grey
Dawn, and the Pleiades before him danced,
Shedding sweet influence: Less bright the moon,
But opposite in levelled west was set
His mirror, with full face borrowing her light
From him; for other light she needed none
In that aspect, and still that distance keeps
Till night, then in the east her turn she shines,
Revolved on Heaven's great axle; and her reign
With thousand lesser lights dividual holds,
With thousand thousand stars, that then appeared
Spangling the hemisphere.

— John Milton (1608–1674)

VIRGO

23 AUGUST – 22 SEPTEMBER

VIRGO

23 AUGUST – 22 SEPTEMBER

'the touchstone of the conscience'

SYMBOL	MAIDEN
MODALITY	MUTABLE
ELEMENT	EARTH
RULER	MERCURY
POLARITY	NEGATIVE/FEMININE

VIRGO: INTRODUCTION

The last sign of the summer, Virgo is a mutable, feminine earth sign, ruled by Mercury. Virgo is often depicted as a young woman carrying a sheaf of wheat and this makes sense in terms of the cycle of the year, as summer moves towards autumn. Virgo is also associated with Demeter, the Greek goddess of the harvest.

Typical characteristics cluster around a tendency for analysis: articulate, critical and intellectual. Additionally Virgos are practical and hardworking, excelling in craftsmanship and multifaceted skills. When approaching tasks and challenges Virgos are usually observant, insightful and extremely capable. Mercury brings in a sense of restlessness and nervous energy.

Poems for Virgo showcase sophisticated and inventive verse-worlds. They bring an idiosyncratic yet value-laden versatility based on real-life observations and personal experience. These poems approach their subject matter in an analytical rather than romantic way, but they don't lose sight of the abundance of this late summer star sign and its maidenly symbolism.

A MAIDEN

Oh if I were the velvet rose
  Upon the red rose vine,
I'd climb to touch his window
  And make his casement fine.

And if I were the bright-eyed bird
  That twitters on the tree,
All day I'd sing my love for him
  Till he should harken me.

But since I am a maiden
  I go with downcast eyes,
And he will never hear the songs
  That he has turned to sighs.

And since I am a maiden
  My love will never know
That I could kiss him with a mouth
  More red than roses blow.

— Sara Teasdale (1884–1933)

THOUGHT

Thought, I love thought.
But not the juggling and twisting of already existent ideas
I despise that self-important game.
Thought is the welling up of unknown life into consciousness,
Thought is the testing of statements on the touchstone
of the conscience,
Thought is gazing on to the face of life, and reading what
can be read,
Thought is pondering over experience, and coming to
a conclusion.
Thought is not a trick, or an exercise, or a set of dodges,
Thought is a man in his wholeness wholly attending.

– D H Lawrence (1885–1930)

THE BUILDERS

All are architects of Fate,
   Working in these walls of Time;
Some with massive deeds and great,
   Some with ornaments of rhyme.

Nothing useless is, or low;
   Each thing in its place is best;
And what seems but idle show
   Strengthens and supports the rest.

For the structure that we raise,
   Time is with materials filled;
Our to-days and yesterdays
   Are the blocks with which we build.

Truly shape and fashion these;
   Leave no yawning gaps between;
Think not, because no man sees,
   Such things will remain unseen.

In the elder days of Art,
   Builders wrought with greatest care
Each minute and unseen part;
   For the Gods see everywhere.

Let us do our work as well,
   Both the unseen and the seen;
Make the house, where Gods may dwell,
   Beautiful, entire, and clean.

Else our lives are incomplete,
  Standing in these walls of Time,
Broken stairways, where the feet
  Stumble as they seek to climb.

Build to-day, then, strong and sure,
  With a firm and ample base;
And ascending and secure
  Shall to-morrow find its place.

Thus alone can we attain
  To those turrets, where the eye
Sees the world as one vast plain,
  And one boundless reach of sky.

— Henry Wadsworth Longfellow (1807–1882)

TELL ALL THE TRUTH BUT TELL IT SLANT –

Tell all the truth but tell it slant –
Success in Circuit lies
Too bright for our infirm Delight
The Truth's superb surprise
As Lightning to the Children eased
With explanation kind
The Truth must dazzle gradually
Or every man be blind –

– Emily Dickinson (1830–1886)

PERFORMANCE

I starred last night, I shone:
I was footwork and firework in one,

a rocket that wriggled up and shot
darkness with a parasol of brilliants
and a peewee descant on a flung bit;
I was blusters of glitter-bombs expanding
to mantle and aurora from a crown,
I was fouéttes, falls of blazing paint,
para-flares spot-welding cloudy heaven,
loose gold off fierce toeholds of white,
a finale red-tongued as a haka leap:
that too was a butt of all right!

As usual after any triumph, I was
of course inconsolable.

— *Les Murray (1938–2019)*

ON HIS TORN GARMENT

I have a mantle; it resembles a sieve
For sifting wheat or barley;
In the dark of night I unfurl it like a tent
And heavens starry radiance filters through;
I behold the moon and the Pleiades,
Even Orion's lustre is reflected;
I grow weary counting its holes
Like many teeth of a giant saw;
To attempt to sew its shreds
Crosswise is hopeless;
Were a fly to descend on it compulsively
Like a fool, he would regret it!
O God convert this rag to one worthy of praise and repair.

– Abraham Ibn Ezra (1089–1167)
Translated by Leon J. Weinberger

AS YOU GO THROUGH LIFE

Don't look for the flaws as you go through life;
And even when you find them,
It is wise and kind to be somewhat blind,
And look for the virtue behind them;
For the cloudiest night has a hint of light
Somewhere in its shadows hiding;
It's better by far to hunt for a star,
Than the spots on the sun abiding.

The current of life runs ever away
To the bosom of God's great ocean.
Don't set your force 'gainst the river's course,
And think to alter its motion.
Don't waste a curse on the universe,
Remember, it lived before you;
Don't butt at the storm with your puny form,
But bend and let it go o'er you.

The world will never adjust itself
To suit your whims to the letter,
Some things must go wrong your whole life long,
And the sooner you know it the better.
It is folly to fight with the Infinite,
And go under at last in the wrestle.
The wiser man shapes into God's plan
As water shapes into a vessel.

– Ella Wheeler Wilcox (1850–1919)

93 PERCENT STARDUST

We have calcium in our bones,
iron in our veins,
carbon in our souls,
and nitrogen in our brains.
93 percent stardust,
with souls made of flames,
we are all just stars
that have people names.

– Nikita Gill (b. 1987)

HARVEST TIME

Pillowed and hushed on the silent plain,
Wrapped in her mantle of golden grain,

Wearied of pleasuring weeks away,
Summer is lying asleep to-day, –

Where winds come sweet from the wild-rose briers
And the smoke of the far-off prairies fires;

Yellow her hair as the golden rod,
And brown her cheeks as the prairie sod;

Purple her eyes as the mists that dream
At the edge of some laggard sun-drowned stream;

But over their depths the lashes sweep,
For Summer is lying to-day asleep.

The north wind kisses her rosy mouth,
His rival frowns in the far-off south,

And comes caressing her sunburnt cheek,
And Summer awakes for one short week, –

Awakes and gathers her wealth of grain,
Then sleeps and dreams for a year again.

— Emily Pauline Johnson (1861–1913)

LIBRA
23 SEPTEMBER – 22 OCTOBER

LIBRA

23 SEPTEMBER – 22 OCTOBER

'Be not afraid / To thrust aside half-truths and grasp the whole'

SYMBOL	SCALES
MODALITY	CARDINAL
ELEMENT	AIR
RULER	VENUS
POLARITY	POSITIVE/MASCULINE

LIBRA: INTRODUCTION

We now move from the summer star signs to those of autumn: to Libra, Scorpio and Sagittarius. Libra is the third cardinal star sign and, like Aries and Cancer, this powerful characteristic puts it at the head of a new season. Governed by the element of air, it almost feels like Libra must be the originator of the gusts and winds of the autumnal months, clearing the way for winter and after that the cycle to begin again. Air signs are often seen as intellectual: Gemini is ruled by quick-witted Mercury; but Libra, governed by Venus, the goddess of love, creates a different nuance, perhaps in the Librans' use of their skills to foster harmony and social connection.

Represented as the scales, Libra is the only abstract symbol of the zodiac. The symbol clearly relates to the notion of inner balance and harmonious relations with others.

Librans' ability to understand both sides of a situation can lead to protracted indecision, but they are driven by a belief in fairness and in acting rationally. With Venus as part of their unique equation, they are also romantic, charming, easy-going and sociable with an extra dose of idealism and sensibility.

Poems for Libra remind us that there is more than one way of looking at the world and that having a sense of perspective is something that we all should learn to value whether we are faced with a decision to take, a new encounter to evaluate or a challenging situation to navigate. These poems express and explore diversity, for we are not journeying through this life on our own. They draw us to our interconnectedness and the importance of reaching for harmony rather than creating discord.

A HYMN TO VENUS

Extract

O Venus, beauty of the skies,
To whom a thousand temples rise,
Gayly false in gentle smiles,
Full of love-perplexing wiles,
O goddess! from my heart remove
The wasting cares and pains of love.

If ever thou hast kindly heard
A song in soft distress preferred,
Propitious to my tuneful vow,
O gentle goddess! hear me now.
Descend thou bright, immortal, guest,
In all thy radiant charms confessed.
...

Celestial visitant, once more
Thy needful presence I implore!
In pity come, and ease my grief,
Bring my distempered soul relief:
Favour thy suppliant's hidden fires,
And give me all my heart desires.

– Sappho (c. 630–c. 570 BCE)
Translated by Ambrose Philips

SHOOTING THE SUN

Four horizons cozen me
To distances I dimly see.
Four paths beckon me to stray,
Each a bold and separate way.
Monday morning shows the East
Satisfying as a feast.
Tuesday I will none of it,
West alone holds benefit.
Later in the week 'tis due
North that I would hurry to.
While on other days I find
To the South content of mind.
So I start, but never rest
North or South or East or West.
Each horizon has its claim
Solace to a different aim.
Four-soul'd like the wind am I,
Voyaging an endless sky,
Undergoing destiny.

— Amy Lowell (1874–1925)

NO MAN IS AN ISLAND

From *Devotions upon Emergent Occasions*

No man is an island,
Entire of itself,
Every man is a piece of the continent,
A part of the main.
If a clod be washed away by the sea,
Europe is the less.
As well as if a promontory were.
As well as if a manor of thy friend's
Or of thine own were:
Any man's death diminishes me,
Because I am involved in mankind,
And therefore never send to know for whom the bell tolls;
It tolls for thee.

— John Donne (1572–1631)

THE ROAD NOT TAKEN

Two roads diverged in a yellow wood,
And sorry I could not travel both
And be one traveler, long I stood
And looked down one as far as I could
To where it bent in the undergrowth;

Then took the other, as just as fair,
And having perhaps the better claim,
Because it was grassy and wanted wear;
Though as for that the passing there
Had worn them really about the same,

And both that morning equally lay
In leaves no step had trodden black.
Oh, I kept the first for another day!
Yet knowing how way leads on to way,
I doubted if I should ever come back.

I shall be telling this with a sigh
Somewhere ages and ages hence:
Two roads diverged in a wood, and I –
I took the one less traveled by,
And that has made all the difference.

— Robert Frost (1874–1963)

A CHARACTER

I marvel how Nature could ever find space
For so many strange contrasts in one human face:
There's thought and no thought, and there's paleness
   and bloom
And bustle and sluggishness, pleasure and gloom.

There's weakness, and strength both redundant and vain;
Such strength as, if ever affliction and pain
Could pierce through a temper that's soft to disease,
Would be rational peace - a philosopher's ease.

There's indifference, alike when he fails or succeeds,
And attention full ten times as much as there needs;
Pride where there's no envy, there's so much of joy;
And mildness, and spirit both forward and coy.

There's freedom, and sometimes a diffident stare
Of shame scarcely seeming to know that she's there,
There's virtue, the title it surely may claim,
Yet wants heaven knows what to be worthy the name.

This picture from nature may seem to depart,
Yet the Man would at once run away with your heart;
And I for five centuries right gladly would be
Such an odd such a kind happy creature as he.

— *William Wordsworth (1770–1850)*

PROGRESS

Let there be many windows to your soul,
That all the glory of the universe
May beautify it. Not the narrow pane
Of one poor creed can catch the radiant rays
That shine from countless sources. Tear away
The blinds of superstition; let the light
Pour through fair windows broad as Truth itself
And high as God.

Why should the spirit peer
Through some priest-curtained orifice, and grope
Along dim corridors of doubt, when all
The splendour from unfathomed seas of space
Might bathe it with the golden waves of Love?
Sweep up the débris of decaying faiths;
Sweep down the cobwebs of worn-out beliefs,
And throw your soul wide open to the light
Of Reason and of Knowledge. Tune your ear
To all the wordless music of the stars
And to the voice of Nature, and your heart
Shall turn to truth and goodness, as the plant
Turns to the sun. A thousand unseen hands
Reach down to help you to their peace-crowned heights.
And all the forces of the firmament
Shall fortify your strength. Be not afraid
To thrust aside half-truths and grasp the whole.

— Ella Wheeler Wilcox (1850–1919)

FOR WHO KNOWS ALL THAT KNOWLEDGE CONTAINS?

Extract from *Hudibras*

For who knows all that knowledge contains?
Men dwell not on the tops of mountains,
But on their sides, or rising's seat;
So 'tis with knowledge's vast height.
Do not the hist'ries of all ages
Relate miraculous presages
Of strange turns in the world's affairs,
Foreseen b' astrologers, soothsayers,
Chaldeans, learn'd Genethliacks,
And some that have writ almanacks?

– Samuel Butler (1612–1680)

AUGURIES OF INNOCENCE

Extract

To see a World in a grain of sand,
And a Heaven in a wild flower,
Hold Infinity in the palm of your hand,
And Eternity in an hour.
A robin redbreast in a cage
Puts all Heaven in a rage.
A dove-house fill'd with doves and pigeons
Shudders Hell thro' all its regions.
A dog starv'd at his master's gate
Predicts the ruin of the State.
A horse misus'd upon the road
Calls to Heaven for human blood.
Each outcry of the hunted hare
A fibre from the brain does tear.
A skylark wounded in the wing,
A cherubim does cease to sing.
The game-cock clipt and arm'd for fight
Does the rising sun affright.
Every wolf's and lion's howl
Raises from Hell a Human soul.
The wild deer, wandering here and there,
Keeps the Human soul from care.
...
The bleat, the bark, the bellow, and roar
Are waves that beat on Heaven's shore.
...

Every night and every morn
Some to misery are born.
Every morn and every night
Some are born to sweet delight.
Some are born to sweet delight,
Some are born to endless night.
We are led to believe a lie
When we see not thro' the eye
Which was born in a night to perish in a night,
When the Soul slept in beams of light.
God appears and God is Light
To those poor souls who dwell in Night,
But does a Human Form display
To those who dwell in realms of Day.

— William Blake (1757–1827)

TO EVERY THING THERE IS A SEASON

Ecclesiastes 3:1–8

To every thing there is a season, and a time to every
purpose under the heaven:
A time to be born, and a time to die; a time to plant,
and a time to pluck up that which is planted;
A time to kill, and a time to heal; a time to break down,
and a time to build up,
A time to weep, and a time to laugh; a time to mourn,
and a time to dance;
A time to cast away stones, and a time to gather stones
together; a time to embrace, and a time to refrain
from embracing;
A time to get, and a time to lose; a time to keep,
and a time to cast away;
A time to rend, and a time to sew; a time to keep silence,
and a time to speak;
A time to love, and a time to hate; a time of war,
and a time of peace.

— *King James translation*

SCORPIO
23 OCTOBER – 21 NOVEMBER

SCORPIO

23 OCTOBER – 21 NOVEMBER

'I am the captain of my soul'

SYMBOL	SCORPION
MODALITY	FIXED
ELEMENT	WATER
RULER	MARS/PLUTO
POLARITY	NEGATIVE/FEMININE

SCORPIO: INTRODUCTION

Scorpio is the eighth sign of the zodiac. Those born under this star sign are often passionate, intense, determined and loyal. Not only do they have a strong inner core, they have potential to create transformations. Their intensity stems from a profound, unmoving emotional depth, which is reflective of the combined quality of being a water sign as well as a fixed modality. Their inner control is legendary.

It is the only sign of the zodiac that has three symbols representing it: the scorpion (primarily), the eagle and the phoenix. Scorpios are co-ruled by Mars and Pluto.

Poems for Scorpio exude passion and intensity and soar with wonder. They describe states and processes of transformation, like that of the phoenix. They feature the planet Mars, and the colour red; and range over the depths and expanse of the universe. Readers will be inspired by the determination and resilience at the heart of the poems: their words might even set off real-world transformation.

THE POWERS OF THE MIND

From the Latin poem *Astronomica*, Book I

No barriers, no masses of matter,
however enormous,
can withstand the powers of the mind
the remotest corners yield to them;
all things succumb,
the very heaven itself is laid open.

– Marcus Manilius (1st century CE)

PHOENIX

Are you willing to be sponged out, erased, cancelled,
made nothing?
Are you willing to be made nothing?
dipped into oblivion?

If not, you will never really change.

The phoenix renews her youth
only when she is burnt, burnt alive, burnt down
to hot and flocculent ash.
Then the small stirring of a new small bub in the nest
with strands of down like floating ash
Shows that she is renewing her youth like the eagle,
Immortal bird.

– D H Lawrence (1885–1930)

GOD'S WORLD

O world, I cannot hold thee close enough!
   Thy winds, thy wide grey skies!
   Thy mists, that roll and rise!
Thy woods, this autumn day, that ache and sag
And all but cry with colour! That gaunt crag
To crush! To lift the lean of that black bluff!
World, World, I cannot get thee close enough!

Long have I known a glory in it all,
   But never knew I this;
   Here such a passion is
As stretcheth me apart, – Lord, I do fear
Thou'st made the world too beautiful this year;
My soul is all but out of me, – let fall
No burning leaf; prithee, let no bird call.

— Edna St Vincent Millay (1892–1950)

INVICTUS

Out of the night that covers me,
Black as the pit from pole to pole,
I thank whatever gods may be
For my unconquerable soul.

In the fell clutch of circumstance
I have not winced nor cried aloud.
Under the bludgeonings of chance
My head is bloody, but unbowed.

Beyond this place of wrath and tears
Looms but the Horror of the shade,
And yet the menace of the years
Finds and shall find me unafraid.

It matters not how strait the gate,
How charged with punishments the scroll,
I am the master of my fate:
I am the captain of my soul.

– William Ernest Henley (1849–1903)

MARS BEING RED

Being red is the color of a white sun where it lingers
on an arm. Color of time lost in sparks, of space lost
inside dance. Red of walks by the railroad in the flush
of youth, while our steps released the squeaks
of shoots reaching for the light. Scarlet of sin, crimson
of fresh blood, ruby and garnet of the jewel bed,
early sunshine, vestiges of the late sun as it turns
green and disappears. Be calm. Do not give in
to the rabid red throat of age. In a red world, imprint
the valentine and blush of romance for the dark.
It has come. You will not be this quick-to-redden
forever. You will be green again, again and again.

– Marvin Bell (1937–2020)

OPTIMISM

More and more I have come to admire resilience.
Not the simple resistance of a pillow, whose foam
returns over and over to the same shape, but the sinuous
tenacity of a tree: finding the light newly blocked on one side,
it turns in another. A blind intelligence, true.
But out of such persistence arose turtles, rivers,
mitochondria, figs – all this resinous, unretractable earth.

– Jane Hirshfield (b. 1953)

BRIGHT STAR! WOULD I WERE STEADFAST AS THOU ART

Bright star! would I were steadfast as thou art –
Not in lone splendour hung aloft the night,
And watching, with eternal lids apart,
Like nature's patient, sleepless Eremite,
The moving waters at their priestlike task
Of pure ablution round earth's human shores,
Or gazing on the new soft fallen mask
Of snow upon the mountains and the moors –
No – yet still steadfast, still unchangeable,
Pillow'd upon my fair love's ripening breast,
To feel for ever its soft fall and swell,
Awake for ever in a sweet unrest,
Still, still to hear her tender-taken breath,
And so live ever – or else swoon to death.

— John Keats (1795–1821)

STILL I RISE

You may write me down in history
With your bitter, twisted lies,
You may trod me in the very dirt
But still, like dust, I'll rise.

Does my sassiness upset you?
Why are you beset with gloom?
'Cause I walk like I've got oil wells
Pumping in my living room.

Just like moons and like suns,
With the certainty of tides,
Just like hopes springing high,
Still I'll rise.

Did you want to see me broken?
Bowed head and lowered eyes?
Shoulders falling down like teardrops,
Weakened by my soulful cries?

Does my haughtiness offend you?
Don't you take it awful hard
'Cause I laugh like I've got gold mines
Diggin' in my own backyard.

You may shoot me with your words,
You may cut me with your eyes,
You may kill me with your hatefulness,
But still, like air, I'll rise.

Does my sexiness upset you?
Does it come as a surprise
That I dance like I've got diamonds
At the meeting of my thighs?

Out of the huts of history's shame
I rise
Up from a past that's rooted in pain
I rise
I'm a black ocean, leaping and wide,
Welling and swelling I bear in the tide.

Leaving behind nights of terror and fear
I rise
Into a daybreak that's wondrously clear
I rise
Bringing the gifts that my ancestors gave,
I am the dream and the hope of the slave.
I rise
I rise
I rise.

– Maya Angelou (1928–2014)

NATURE, THAT FRAM'D US OF FOUR ELEMENTS

From *Tamburlaine the Great, Part I,* Act II, scene vi

Nature, that fram'd us of four elements
Warring within our breasts for regiment.
Doth teach us all to have aspiring minds:
Our souls, whose faculties can comprehend
The wondrous architecture of the world,
And measure every wandering planet's course.
Still climbing after knowledge infinite,
And always moving as the restless spheres.

– Christopher Marlowe (1564–1593)

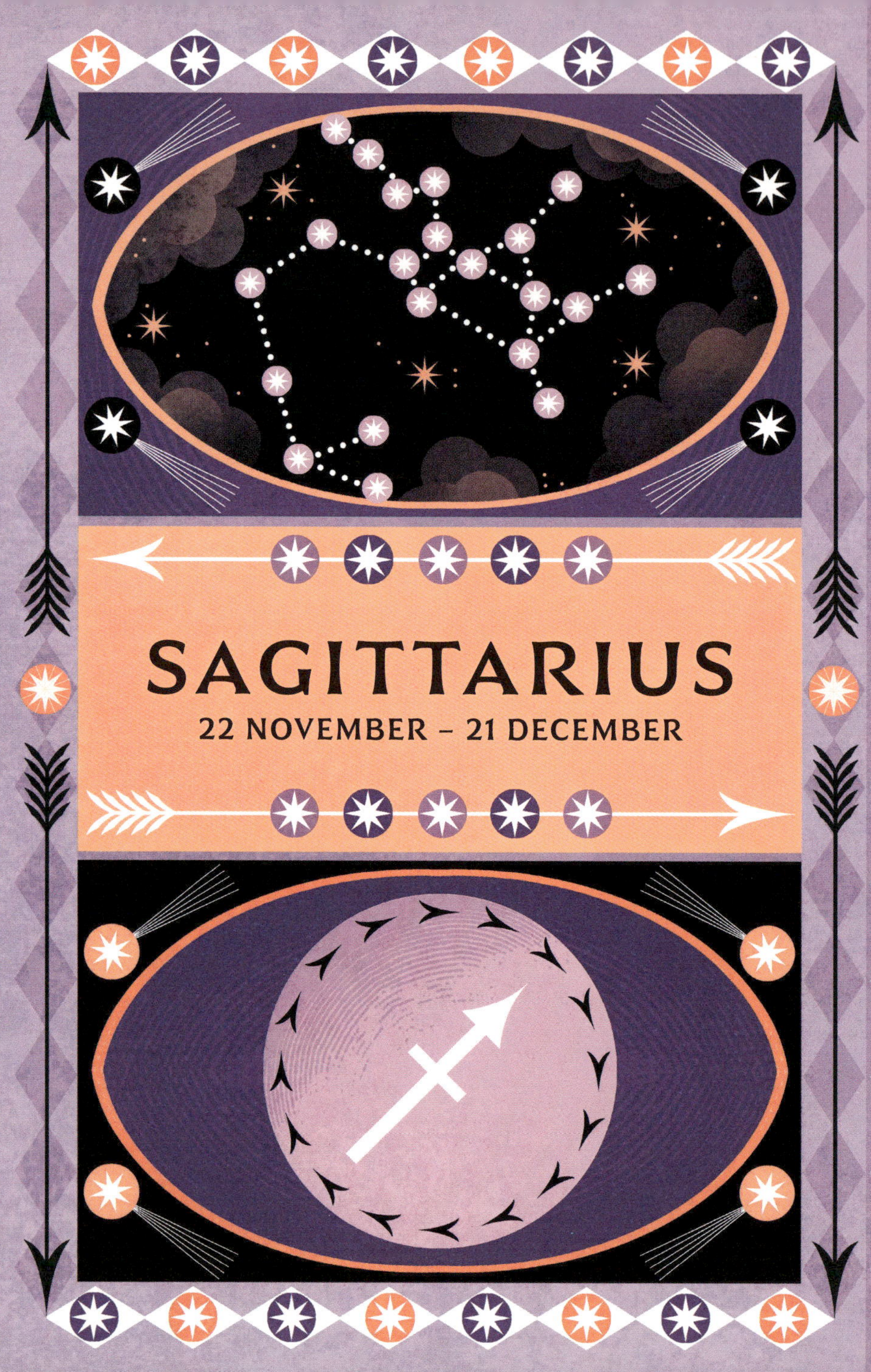
SAGITTARIUS
22 NOVEMBER – 21 DECEMBER

SAGITTARIUS

22 NOVEMBER – 21 DECEMBER

'With sounding hoofs across the earth I fly'

SYMBOL	ARCHER
MODALITY	MUTABLE
ELEMENT	FIRE
RULER	JUPITER
POLARITY	POSITIVE/MASCULINE

SAGITTARIUS: INTRODUCTION

Sagittarius, the ninth sign of the zodiac, is the last of the fire signs. It is ruled by the planet Jupiter. Those born under this star sign strive to discover the meaning of existence, so often turn to religion or philosophy for guidance. They remain firm, positive and undeterred in attempting to fulfil such an elusive goal.

Sagittarius is the sign of the seeker: adventurous, independent by nature, energetic and filled with a sense of possibility. The Sagittarian sense of self is at its most realized when they are exploring the world, wondering and wandering. Their sense of curiosity knows no bounds, and with that comes optimism and open-mindedness.

Sagittarius is the Latin word for archer and is usually depicted as a centaur (part-man/part-horse) holding a bow and arrow.

Poems for Sagittarius seek a deeper truth while exuding optimism and a strong and resilient spirit that feel like they are communicating faith in oneself and the world. Here the reader will find curiosity without cynicism; purposeful action accompanied by thoughtfulness; philosophical exploration without preaching.

THE CENTAUR, SAGITTARIUS, AM I

From *The Poet's Calendar*

The Centaur, Sagittarius, am I,
 Born of Ixion's and the cloud's embrace;
With sounding hoofs across the earth I fly,
 A steed Thessalian with a human face.
Sharp winds the arrows are with which I chase
 The leaves, half dead already with affright;
I shroud myself in gloom; and to the race
 Of mortals bring nor comfort nor delight.

– Henry Wadsworth Longfellow (1807–1882)

LIFE

Let me but live my life from year to year,
   With forward face and unreluctant soul;
   Not hurrying to, nor turning from, the goal;
Not mourning for the things that disappear
In the dim past, nor holding back in fear
   From what the future veils; but with a whole
   And happy heart, that pays its toll
To Youth and Age, and travels on with cheer.

So let the way wind up the hill or down,
   O'er rough or smooth, the journey will be joy:
   Still seeking what I sought when but a boy,
New friendship, high adventure, and a crown,
My heart will keep the courage of the quest,
And hope the road's last turn will be the best.

– Henry Van Dyke (1852–1933)

IN THE SEVEN WOODS

I have heard the pigeons of the Seven Woods
Make their faint thunder, and the garden bees
Hum in the lime-tree flowers; and put away
The unavailing outcries and the old bitterness
That empty the heart. I have forgot awhile
Tara uprooted, and new commonness
Upon the throne and crying about the streets
And hanging its paper flowers from post to post,
Because it is alone of all things happy.
I am contented, for I know that Quiet
Wanders laughing and eating her wild heart
Among pigeons and bees, while that Great Archer,
Who but awaits His hour to shoot, still hangs
A cloudy quiver over Parc-na-lee.

— W B Yeats (1865–1939)

THE STORY

I knew that it lay about me,
I knew that the story I had to live was near
But fenced off. Only I
Could find the entrance, and not by straining and
fighting
But only, always by

Being prepared for the great surrender, the huge
Advance and appearance. Nothing to do with fear
Was this. I only had
To let the four seasons march in order ahead,
To watch the sky changing and meeting the sea.
This was the way I had to let things happen,
To let the world appear
In all its golden finish and lucky end.
I watched the door of morning start to open,
I simply put out my hand.

— Elizabeth Jennings (1926–2001)

BUT I CAN'T

Time will say nothing but I told you so,
Time only knows the price we have to pay;
If I could tell you I would let you know.

If we should weep when clowns put on their show,
If we should stumble when musicians play,
Time will say nothing but I told you so.

There are no fortunes to be told, although,
Because I love you more than I can say,
If I could tell you I would let you know.

The winds must come from somewhere when they blow,
There must be reason why the leaves decay;
Time will say nothing but I told you so.

Perhaps the roses really want to grow,
The vision seriously intends to stay;
If I could tell you I would let you know.

Suppose the lions all get up and go,
And the brooks and soldiers run away;
Will Time say nothing but I told you so?
If I could tell you I would let you know.

— W H Auden (1907–1973)

THE BURIED LIFE

Extract

But often, in the world's most crowded streets,
But often, in the din of strife,
There rises an unspeakable desire
After the knowledge of our buried life,
A thirst to spend our fire and restless force
In tracking out our true, original course;
A longing to inquire
Into the mystery of this heart which beats
So wild, so deep in us, to know
Whence our lives come and where they go.
...
A bolt is shot back somewhere in our breast
And a lost pulse of feeling stirs again:
The eye sinks inward, and the heart lies plain,
And what we mean, we say, and what we would, we know.
A man becomes aware of his life's flow,
And hears its winding murmur, and he sees
The meadows where it glides, the sun, the breeze.

— Matthew Arnold (1822–1888)

HOROSCOPE

Again the white blanket
icicles pierce.
The fierce teeth
of steel-framed snowshoes
bite the trail open.
Where the hardwoods stand
and rarely bend
the wind blows hard
an explosion of snow
like flour dusting
the baker in a shop
long since shuttered.
In this our post-shame century
we will reclaim
the old nouns
unembarrassed.
If it rains
we'll say oh
there's rain.
If she falls
out of love
with you you'll carry
your love on a gold plate
to the forest and bury it
in the Indian graveyard.
Pioneers do not
only despoil.
The sweet knees

of oxen have pressed
a path for me.
A lone chickadee
undaunted thing
sings in the snow.
Flakes appear
as if out of air
but surely they come
from somewhere
bearing what news
from the troposphere.
The sky's shifted
and Capricorns abandon
themselves to a Sagittarian
line. I like
this weird axis.
In 23,000 years
it will become again
the same sky
the Babylonians scanned.

– Maureen N McLane (b. 1967)

THE PITCHFORK

Of all implements, the pitchfork was the one
That came near to an imagined perfection:
When he tightened his raised hand and aimed with it,
It felt like a javelin, accurate and light.

So whether he played the warrior or the athlete
Or worked in earnest in the chaff and sweat,
He loved its grain of tapering, dark-flecked ash
Grown satiny from its own natural polish.

Riveted steel, turned timber, burnish, grain,
Smoothness, straightness, roundness, length and sheen.
Sweat-cured, sharpened, balanced, tested, fitted.
The springiness, the clip and dart of it.

And then when he thought of probes that reached the farthest,
He would see the shaft of a pitchfork sailing past
Evenly, imperturbably through space,
Its prongs starlit and absolutely soundless –

But has learned at last to follow that simple lead
Past its own aim, out to another side
Where perfection – or nearness to it – is imagined
Not in the aiming but the opening hand.

– Seamus Heaney (1939–2013)

WHEN I HEARD THE LEARN'D ASTRONOMER

When I heard the learn'd astronomer;
When the proofs, the figures, were ranged in columns
before me;
When I was shown the charts and diagrams, to add, divide,
and measure them;
When I, sitting, heard the astronomer, where he lectured
with much applause in the lecture-room,
How soon, unaccountable, I became tired and sick;
Till rising and gliding out, I wander'd off by myself,
In the mystical moist night-air, and from time to time,
Look'd up in perfect silence at the stars.

– Walt Whitman (1819–1892)

CAPRICORN

22 DECEMBER – 19 JANUARY

CAPRICORN

22 DECEMBER – 19 JANUARY

'We must arise and go'

SYMBOL	GOAT
MODALITY	CARDINAL
ELEMENT	EARTH
RULER	SATURN
POLARITY	NEGATIVE/FEMININE

CAPRICORN: INTRODUCTION

The final cardinal sign, Capricorn ushers in the last of the seasons: the winter months, with associated star signs Aquarius and Pisces completing the season and the zodiac year. Capricorn is a feminine earth sign, ruled by Saturn.

Capricorn's duality is symbolized by a creature that is half-goat and half-fish. The goat, which clambers and climbs up the steep mountain of success, is ambitious, cautious and hard-working. The fish, in contrast to the goat's ascent, swims in the depths, adding a touch of the unknowable and a sensitive side.

Capricorns' ambitious natures come with a strong sense of duty and the need to take on responsibility. They are upholders of tradition and protectors of civilization. This outlook needs to go hand-in-hand with deep compassion as well as an approach that is prudent and practical. The outcome of this can lead Capricorns to be serious, even stern.

Poems for Capricorn see the world for what it is, and recognize not only its beauty but its spectrum of complexity. Here is rhythm, movement and action. Yet individual responsibility for the goal-oriented Capricorn is at the heart of these poems. The way forward may not be easy or straightforward or even knowable, but these poems help focus the mind, offer reassurance and aim to galvanize the reader into action.

EARTH'S EMBROIDERY

With the ink of its showers and rains,
with the quill of its lightning,
with the hand of its clouds,
winter wrote a letter upon the garden, in purple and blue.
No artist could ever conceive the like of that.
And this is why the earth, grown jealous of the sky,
embroidered stars in the folds of the flower-beds.

– Solomon Ibn Gabirol (c. 1022–c. 1070)
Translated by T Carmi

A WALK

My eyes already touch the sunny hill,
going far ahead of the road I have begun.
So we are grasped by what we cannot grasp;
it has an inner light, even from a distance –

and changes us, even if we do not reach it,
into something else, which, hardly sensing it, we
  already are;
a gesture waves us on, answering our own wave…
but what we feel is the wind in our faces.

— Rainer Maria Rilke (1875–1926)
Translated by Robert Bly

THE RUBAIYAT OF OMAR KHAYYAM

Verses 31–33

Up from Earth's Center through the Seventh Gate
I rose, and on the Throne of Saturn sate,
   And many a Knot unravel'd by the Road;
But not the Master-knot of Human Fate.

There was the Door to which I found no Key;
There was the Veil through which I might not see:
   Some little talk awhile of ME and THEE
There was - and then no more of THEE and ME.

Earth could not answer; nor the Seas that mourn
In flowing Purple, of their Lord Forlorn;
   Nor rolling Heaven, with all his Signs reveal'd
And hidden by the sleeve of Night and Morn.

– Omar Khayyam (1048–1131)
Translated by Edward Fitzgerald (1809–1883)

THE WAY IT IS

There's a thread you follow. It goes among
things that change. But it doesn't change.
People wonder about what you are pursuing.
You have to explain about the thread.
But it is hard for others to see.
While you hold it you can't get lost.
Tragedies happen; people get hurt
or die; and you suffer and get old.
Nothing you do can stop time's unfolding.
You don't ever let go of the thread.

– William Stafford (1914–1993)

THE WILD GOAT

O you would clothe me in silken frocks
   And house me from the cold,
And bind with bright bands my glossy locks,
   And buy me chains of gold.

And give me, meekly to do my will,
   The hapless sons of men;
But the wild goat bounding on the barren hill
   Droops in the grassy pen.

– Claude McKay (1889–1948)

TRY TO PRAISE THE MUTILATED WORLD

Try to praise the mutilated world.
Remember June's long days,
and wild strawberries, drops of rosé wine.
The nettles that methodically overgrow
the abandoned homesteads of exiles.
You must praise the mutilated world.
You watched the stylish yachts and ships;
one of them had a long trip ahead of it,
while salty oblivion awaited others.
You've seen the refugees going nowhere,
you've heard the executioners sing joyfully.
You should praise the mutilated world.
Remember the moments when we were together
in a white room and the curtain fluttered.
Return in thought to the concert where music flared.
You gathered acorns in the park in autumn
and leaves eddied over the earth's scars.
Praise the mutilated world
and the gray feather a thrush lost,
and the gentle light that strays and vanishes
and returns.

– Adam Zagajewski (1945–2021)
Translated by Clare Cavanagh

DELAY

The radiance of that star that leans on me
Was shining years ago. The light that now
Glitters up there my eyes may never see,
And so the time lag teases me with how

Love that loves now may not reach me until
Its first desire is spent. The star's impulse
Must wait for eyes to claim it beautiful
And love arrived may find us somewhere else.

– Elizabeth Jennings (1926–2001)

THE CALL

From our low seat beside the fire
Where we have dozed and dreamed and watched the glow
Or raked the ashes, stopping so
We scarcely saw the sun or rain
Above, or looked much higher
Than this same quiet red or burned-out fire.
To-night we heard a call,
A rattle on the window-pane,
A voice on the sharp air,
And felt a breath stirring our hair,
A flame within us: Something swift and tall
Swept in and out and that was all.
Was it a bright or a dark angel? Who can know?
It left no mark upon the snow,
But suddenly it snapped the chain
Unbarred, flung wide the door
Which will not shut again;
And so we cannot sit here any more.
We must arise and go:
The world is cold without
And dark and hedged about
With mystery and enmity and doubt,
But we must go
Though yet we do not know
Who called, or what marks we shall leave upon the snow.

– Charlotte Mew (1869–1928)

IF I CAN STOP ONE HEART FROM BREAKING

If I can stop one heart from breaking,
I shall not live in vain;
If I can ease one life the aching,
Or cool one pain,
Or help one fainting robin
Unto his nest again,
I shall not live in vain.

— Emily Dickinson (1830–1886)

MOTHER TO SON

Well, son, I'll tell you:
Life for me ain't been no crystal stair.
It's had tacks in it,
And splinters,
And boards torn up,
And places with no carpet on the floor –
Bare.
But all the time
I'se been a-climbin' on,
And reachin' landin's,
And turnin' corners,
And sometimes goin' in the dark
Where there ain't been no light.
So boy, don't you turn back.
Don't you set down on the steps
'Cause you finds it's kinder hard.
Don't you fall now –
For I'se still goin', honey,
I'se still climbin',
And life for me ain't been no crystal stair.

— *Langston Hughes (1902–1967)*

AQUARIUS

20 JANUARY – 18 FEBRUARY

AQUARIUS

20 JANUARY – 18 FEBRUARY

'Where the mind is without fear and the head is held high'

SYMBOL	WATER–BEARER
MODALITY	FIXED
ELEMENT	AIR
RULER	SATURN/URANUS
POLARITY	POSITIVE/MASCULINE

AQUARIUS: INTRODUCTION

Aquarius is the last of the three intellectual air signs, and is ruled nowadays by the planet Uranus. Uranus, taking its name from the ancient Greek sky god, symbolizes sudden change, flashes of insight and the breaking down of old structures to make way for the new.

Freedom, liberation and innovation are the buzz words here. Those born under this star sign are often humanitarians, progressive in outlook, visionary and inventive. But there is also a sense here not only of community but also individualism and how the two interact. At times loyal and honest, they can also be aloof or unpredictable. Aquarius is represented as the water-bearer, a man or woman pouring water from an amphora or vessel, symbolizing how Aquarians, like the stream of water from the jug, aim to release benefits for the good of all.

Poems for Aquarius celebrate independence and the free spirit (and fresh water, such an essential element of our world). They talk – convincingly, hopefully, powerfully – of seeking freedom and the desire to break down barriers. The individuality of the Aquarius sign is reflected in the diversity of authorial voice and breadth of outlook across the selection aimed at appealing to all readers.

NOW WHEN THE CHEERLESS EMPIRE OF THE SKY

From *Winter*

Now when the cheerless empire of the sky
To Capricorn the Centaur Archer yields,
And fierce Aquarius stains th' inverted year;
Hung o'er the farthest verge of heaven, the sun
Scarce spreads o'er ether the dejected day.
Faint are his gleams, and ineffectual shoot
His struggling rays, in horizontal lines,
Thro' the thick air; as cloth'd in cloudy storm,
Weak, wan, and broad, he skirts the southern sky;
And, soon descending, to the long dark night,
Wide-shading all, the prostrate world resigns.
Nor is the night unwish'd; while vital heat,
Light, life, and joy, the dubious day forsake.
Meantime, in sable cincture, shadows vast,
Deep-ting'ed and damp, and congregated clouds,
And all the vapoury turbulence of heaven,
Involve the face of things. Thus Winter falls

— James Thomson (1700–1748)

THE EARTH IS ALL BEFORE ME

From *The Prelude*, Book 1

The earth is all before me. With a heart
Joyous, nor scared at its own liberty,
I look about; and should the chosen guide
Be nothing better than a wandering cloud,
I cannot miss my way. I breathe again!

— William Wordsworth (1770–1850)

WHERE WATER COMES TOGETHER WITH OTHER WATER

I love creeks and the music they make.
And rills, in glades and meadows, before
they have a chance to become creeks.
I may even love them best of all
for their secrecy. I almost forgot
to say something about the source!
Can anything be more wonderful than a spring?
But the big streams have my heart too.
And the places streams flow into rivers.
The open mouths of rivers where they join the sea.
The places where water comes together
with other water. Those places stand out
in my mind like holy places.
But these coastal rivers!
I love them the way some men love horses
or glamorous women. I have a thing
for this cold swift water.
Just looking at it makes my blood run
and my skin tingle. I could sit
and watch these rivers for hours.
Not one of them like any other.
I'm 45 years old today.
Would anyone believe it if I said
I was once 35?
My heart empty and sere at 35!
Five more years had to pass

before it began to flow again.
I'll take all the time I please this afternoon
before leaving my place alongside this river.
It pleases me, loving rivers.
Loving them all the way back
to their source.
Loving everything that increases me.

– Raymond Carver (1938–1988)

WHERE THE MIND IS WITHOUT FEAR AND THE HEAD IS HELD HIGH

***Gitanjali* 35**

Where the mind is without fear and the head is held high;
Where knowledge is free;
Where the world has not been broken up into fragments by narrow domestic walls;
Where words come out from the depth of truth;
Where tireless striving stretches its arms towards perfection;
Where the clear stream of reason has not lost its way into the dreary desert sand of dead habit;
Where the mind is led forward by thee into ever-widening thought and action –
Into that heaven of freedom, my Father, let my country awake.

– Rabindranath Tagore (1861–1941)

CHOSEN

The lot of love is chosen. I learnt that much
Struggling for an image on the track
Of the whirling Zodiac.
Scarce did he my body touch,
Scarce sank he from the west
Or found a subterranean rest
On the maternal midnight of my breast
Before I had marked him on his northern way,
And seemed to stand although in bed I lay.

I struggled with the horror of daybreak,
I chose it for my lot! If questioned on
My utmost pleasure with a man
By some new-married bride, I take
That stillness for a theme
Where his heart my heart did seem
And both adrift on the miraculous stream
Where – wrote a learned astrologer –
The Zodiac is changed into a sphere.

— *W B Yeats (1865–1939)*

I KNOW MY SOUL

I plucked my soul out of its secret place,
And held it to the mirror of my eye,
To see it like a star against the sky,
A twitching body quivering in space,
A spark of passion shining on my face.
And I explored it to determine why
This awful key to my infinity
Conspires to rob me of sweet joy and grace.
And if the sign may not be fully read,
If I can comprehend but not control,
I need not gloom my days with futile dread,
Because I see a part and not the whole.
Contemplating the strange, I'm comforted
By this narcotic thought: I know my soul.

– Claude McKay (1889–1948)

THE AWAKENING RIVER

The gulls are mad-in-love with the river
And the river unveils her face and smiles.
In her sleep-brooding eyes they mirror their shining wings.
She lies on silver pillows: the sun leans over her.
He warms and warms her, he kisses and kisses her.
There are sparks in her hair and she stirs in laughter.
Be careful, my beautiful waking one! You will catch on fire.
Wheeling and flying with the foam of the sea on their breasts
The ineffable mists of the sea clinging to their wild wings
Crying the rapture of the boundless ocean.
The gulls are mad-in-love with the river.
Wake! we are the dream thoughts flying from your heart.
Wake! we are the songs of desire flowing from your bosom.
O, I think the sun will lend her his great wings
And the river will fly to the sea with the mad-in-love birds.

— *Katherine Mansfield (1888–1923)*

ADDRESS TO MY SOUL

Extract

My soul, be not disturbed
By planetary war;
Remain securely orbed
In this contracted star.

– Elinor Wylie (1885–1928)

SYMPATHY

I know what the caged bird feels, alas!
  When the sun is bright on the upland slopes;
When the wind stirs soft through the springing grass,
And the river flows like a stream of glass;
  When the first bird sings and the first bud opes,
And the faint perfume from its chalice steals –
I know what the caged bird feels!

I know why the caged bird beats his wing
  Till its blood is red on the cruel bars;
For he must fly back to his perch and cling
When he fain would be on the bough a-swing;
  And a pain still throbs in the old, old scars
And they pulse again with a keener sting –
I know why he beats his wing!

I know why the caged bird sings, ah me,
  When his wing is bruised and his bosom sore, –
When he beats his bars and he would be free;
It is not a carol of joy or glee,
  But a prayer that he sends from his heart's deep core,
But a plea, that upward to Heaven he flings –
I know why the caged bird sings!

— Paul Laurence Dunbar (1872–1906)

STAR-TALK

'Are you awake, Gemelli,
This frosty night?'
'We'll be awake till reveillé,
Which is Sunrise,' say the Gemelli,
'It's no good trying to go to sleep:
If there's wine to be got we'll drink it deep,
But sleep is gone for to-night,
But sleep is gone for to-night.'

'Are you cold too, poor Pleiads,
This frosty night?'
'Yes, and so are the Hyads:
See us cuddle and hug,' say the Pleiads,
'All six in a ring: it keeps us warm:
We huddle together like birds in a storm:
It's bitter weather to-night,
It's bitter weather to-night.'

'What do you hunt, Orion,
This starry night?'
'The Ram, the Bull and the Lion,
And the Great Bear,' says Orion,
'With my starry quiver and beautiful belt
I am trying to find a good thick pelt
To warm my shoulders to-night,
To warm my shoulders to-night.'

'Did you hear that, Great She-bear,
This frosty night?'
'Yes, he's talking of stripping *me* bare
Of my own big fur,' says the She-bear,
'I'm afraid of the man and his terrible arrow:
The thought of it chills my bones to the marrow,
And the frost so cruel to-night!
And the frost so cruel to-night!'

'How is your trade, Aquarius,
This frosty night?'
'Complaints is many and various
And my feet are cold,' says Aquarius,
'There's Venus objects to Dolphin-scales,
And Mars to Crab-spawn found in my pails,
And the pump has frozen to-night,
And the pump has frozen to-night.'

— *Robert Graves (1895–1985)*

PISCES

19 FEBRUARY – 20 MARCH

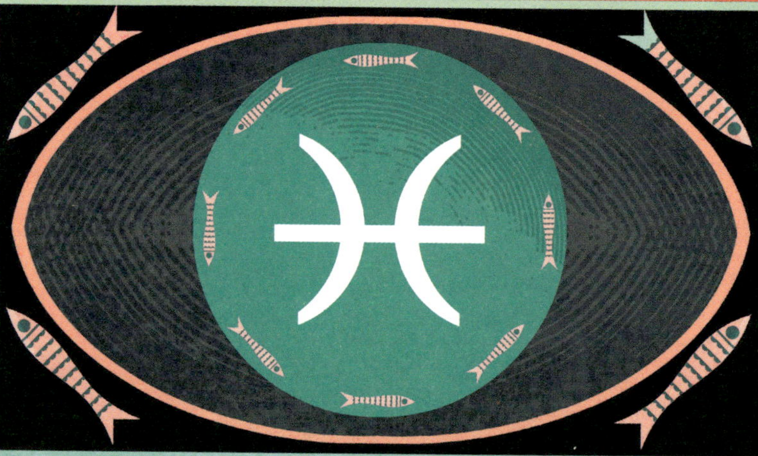

PISCES

19 FEBRUARY – 20 MARCH

'Let your senses and bodies stretch out'

SYMBOL	FISH
MODALITY	MUTABLE
ELEMENT	WATER
RULER	JUPITER/NEPTUNE
POLARITY	NEGATIVE/FEMININE

PISCES: INTRODUCTION

Pisces is the star sign that completes the zodiac wheel. This is the sign of matter and chaos, readying itself for the forthcoming creative burst of Aries and the cycle of the year to begin again. Here boundaries are dissolved, and there is a mythical return to the great ocean from where life once evolved.

Pisces is the sign of dreams and the imagination; of compassion and gentleness and is the most mystical sign of the zodiac. In a sense, it has absorbed all the trials and wisdom of the previous 11 signs. Pisces, a water sign and ruled by Neptune, is symbolized by two fish swimming in opposite directions. Those born under this star sign, as well as being dreamy, are intuitive, wise and empathetic.

Poems for Pisces are oozing with imagination. They evoke dream-like, sometimes liquid landscapes. All poetry takes up physical and imagined space, but this selection seems to expand even beyond these spaces: gazing both inwards and outwards, as well as behind and beyond. Such mysticism is not an add-on, but of the essence to the Pisces in all of us.

ALL THE HEMISPHERES

Leave the familiar for a while.
Let your senses and bodies stretch out

Like a welcomed season
Onto the meadows and shores and hills.

Open up to the Roof.
Make a new water-mark on your excitement
And love.

Like a blooming night flower,
Bestow your vital fragrance of happiness
And giving
Upon our intimate assembly.

Change rooms in your mind for a day.

All the hemispheres in existence
Lie beside an equator
In your heart.

Greet Yourself
In your thousand other forms
As you mount the hidden tide and travel
Back home.

All the hemispheres in heaven
Are sitting around a fire
Chatting

While stitching themselves together
Into the Great Circle inside of
You.

— Hafiz (1310–1390)
Translated by Daniel Ladinsky

FISH

Extract

FISH, oh Fish,
So little matters!

Whether the waters rise and cover the earth
Or whether the waters wilt in the hollow places,
All one to you.

Aqueous, subaqueous,
Submerged
And wave-thrilled.

As the waters roll
Roll you.
The waters wash,
You wash in oneness
And never emerge.

Never know,
Never grasp.

Your life a sluice of sensation along your sides,
A flush at the flails of your fins, down the whorl of
your tail.
And water wetly on fire in the grates of your gills;
Fixed water-eyes.

– D H Lawrence (1885–1930)

ON TIME

From *The Prophet*

And an astronomer said, Master, what of Time?

And he answered:

You would measure time the measureless and the immeasurable.

You would adjust your conduct and even direct the course of your spirit according to hours and seasons.

Of time you would make a stream upon whose bank you would sit and watch its flowing.

Yet the timeless in you is aware of life's timelessness,

And knows that yesterday is but to-day's memory and to-morrow is to-day's dream.

And that that which sings and contemplates in you is still dwelling within the bounds of that first moment which scattered the stars into space.

Who among you does not feel that his power to love is boundless?

And yet who does not feel that very love, though boundless, encompassed within the centre of his being, and moving not from love thought to love thought, nor from love deeds to other love deeds?

And is not time even as love is, undivided and paceless?

But if in your thought you must measure time into seasons, let each season encircle all the other seasons,

And let to-day embrace the past with remembrance and the future with longing.

— *Khalil Gibran (1883–1931)*

POEMS OF JOY

Extract

O to make the most jubilant poems!
O full of music! Full of manhood, womanhood, infancy!
O full of common employments! Full of grain and trees.

O for the voices of animals! O for the swiftness and balance
of fishes!
O for the dropping of rain-drops in a poem!
O for the sunshine, and motion of waves in a poem.

O to be on the sea! the wind, the wide waters around;
O to sail in a ship under full sail at sea.

O the joy of my spirit! It is uncaged! It darts like lightning!
It is not enough to have this globe, or a certain time
- I will have thousands of globes, and all time.

— *Walt Whitman (1819–1892)*

MUSIC

From *Adam Bede*, Chapter 33

Feel its wondrous harmonies

searching the subtlest windings of your soul,
the delicate fibres of life
where no memory can penetrate –

binding together your whole being
past and present
in one unspeakable vibration.

Melting you in one moment
with all the tenderness,
all the love that has been scattered
through the toilsome years.

Concentrating in one emotion
of heroic courage
or resignation
all the hard-learnt lessons
of self-renouncing sympathy,

blending your present joy
with past sorrow –
and your present sorrow
with all your past joy!

— George Eliot (1819–1880)

THE SAME STREAM OF LIFE

***Gitanjali* 69**

The same stream of life that runs through my veins night and day runs through the world and dances in rhythmic measures.

It is the same life that shoots in joy through the dust of the earth in numberless blades of grass and breaks into tumultuous waves of leaves and flowers.

It is the same life that is rocked in the ocean-cradle of birth and of death, in ebb and in flow.

I feel my limbs are made glorious by the touch of this world of life. And my pride is from the life-throb of ages dancing in my blood this moment.

Rabindranath Tagore (1861–1941)

THE FUTURE

Extract

A wanderer is man from his birth.
He was born in a ship
On the breast of the river of Time;
Brimming with wonder and joy
He spreads out his arms to the light,
Rivets his gaze on the banks of the stream.
...
But what was before us we know not,
And we know not what shall succeed.
...
And the width of the waters, the hush
Of the grey expanse where he floats,
Freshening its current and spotted with foam
As it draws to the Ocean, may strike
Peace to the soul of the man on its breast –
As the pale waste widens around him,
As the banks fade dimmer away,
As the stars come out, and the night-wind
Brings up the stream
Murmurs and scents of the infinite sea.

— *Matthew Arnold (1822–1888)*

THE ROYAL CROWN

Extract

Who can know Thy pathways?
For Thou hast made palaces for the seven planets
In the twelve constellations,
And to the Ram and the Bull Thou hast imparted Thy strength in uniting them,
And the third is the Twins, like two brothers in their unity
And their human likeness.
And the fourth is the Crab,
And on him, as on the Lion, hast Thou bestowed of Thy splendour,
And on his sister the Virgin, who is near unto him,
And on the Scales and the Scorpion placed by his side,
And on the ninth that was created in the form of a man of might, whose strength runs not dry,
For he is the Archer, mighty of the bow.
And thus too by Thy great power are created the Goat and the Water-Bearer,
While alone is the last constellation,
'For the Lord did appoint a great Fish.'
And these are the constellations high and exalted in their degrees,
'Twelve princes according to the nations.'

– Solomon ibn Gabirol (c. 1022–c. 1070)
Translated by Israel Zangwill

LISTEN, ALREADY YOU CAN MAKE OUT THE FIRST/RAKINGS OF WORK

From *Sonnets to Orpheus,* Part II
XXV

Listen, already you can make out the first
rakings of work; human rhythm again
heard in the vigorous early spring earth,
its cautious silence. And what is to come

seems reflavoured. What has before
so often come to you seems like the new,
returning. Hoped for always, but never
held in your grasp. It has grasped *you.*

Even the wintered oak trees' leaves
glow an imminent brown in the evening.
Sometimes signs are exchanged in the breeze.

Black, the bushes. But heaps of dung,
lusciously black, collect in the fields.
Every hour that passes grows young.

– Rainer Maria Rilke (1875–1926)
Translated by Marielle Sutherland

INDEX OF POETS

INDEX OF FIRST LINES

SOURCES

"Still I Rise" from AND STILL I RISE: A BOOK OF POEMS by Maya Angelou, copyright © 1978 by Caged Bird Legacy, LLC. Used by permission of Random House, an imprint and division of Penguin Random House LLC. All rights reserved.

Marvin Bell, "Mars Being Red" from Mars Being Red: Poems. Copyright © 2007 by Marvin Bell. Reprinted with the permission of The Permissions Company, LLC on behalf of Copper Canyon Press, coppercanyonpress.org.

From The Penguin Book of Hebrew Verse by T. Carmi published by Penguin Classics. Copyright © T. Carmi, 1981Note on the Systems of Hebrew Versification copyright © Benjamin Hrushovski, 1981. Reprinted by permission of Penguin Books Limited.

From The Penguin Book of Hebrew Verse by T. Carmi published by Penguin Classics. Copyright © T. Carmi, 1981Note on the Systems of Hebrew Versification copyright © Benjamin Hrushovski, 1981. Reprinted by permission of Penguin Books Limited.

Debjani Chatterjee, 'Interludes' from *Namaskar: New & Selected Poems* by Debjani Chatterjee (Redbeck Press, 2004).

THE POEMS OF EMILY DICKINSON, edited by Thomas H. Johnson, Cambridge, Mass.: The Belknap Press of Harvard University Press, Copyright © 1951, 1955 by the President and Fellows of Harvard College. Copyright © renewed 1979, 1983 by the President and Fellows of Harvard College. Copyright © 1914, 1918, 1919, 1924, 1929, 1930, 1932, 1935, 1937, 1942, by Martha Dickinson Bianchi. Copyright © 1952, 1957, 1958, 1963, 1965, by Mary L. Hampson. Used by permission. All rights reserved.

'Star-talk' by Robert Graves (The Complete Poems in One Volume, eds. Beryl Graves and Dunstan Ward, 2000) is reprinted by permission of Carcanet Press on behalf of the Estate of Robert Graves.

"In Spite of Everything, the Stars" from WILD GRATITUDE by Edward Hirsch, copyright © 1981 by Edward Hirsch. Used by permission of Alfred A. Knopf, an imprint of the Knopf Doubleday Publishing Group, a division of Penguin Random House LLC. All rights reserved.

"All the Hemispheres," from The Subject Tonight is Love: 60 Wild and Sweet Poems Inspired by Hafiz by Daniel Ladinsky © 2003 with permission. www.danielladinsky.com.

"My Brilliant Image," from I Heard God Laughing: Poems of Hope and Joy by Daniel Ladinsky 1996, 2006 © with permission. www.danielladinsky.com.

Copyright © 1994 by The Estate of Langston Hughes Reprinted by permission of Harold Ober Associates and International Literary Properties LLC.

Denise Levertov, "Variation on a Theme by Rilke" from Breathing the Water: Poems. Copyright © 1984, 1985, 1986, 1987 by Denise Levertov. Reprinted with the permission of The Permissions Company, LLC, on behalf of New Directions Publishing Corp., ndbooks.com.

Denise Levertov New Selected Poems (Bloodaxe Books, 2003). Reproduced with permission of Bloodaxe Books. www.bloodaxebooks.com @bloodaxebooks (twitter/ facebook) #bloodaxebooks

The Planets by C.S. Lewis copyright © 1935 C.S. Lewis Pte. Ltd. Extract reprinted by permission.

"As Once the Winged Energy of Delight," translation copyright © 1982 by Stephen Mitchell; from SELECTED POETRY OF RAINER MARIA RILKE by Rainer Maria Rilke, edited and translated by Stephen Mitchell. Used by permission of Random House, an imprint and division of Penguin Random House LLC. All rights reserved.

© Pablo Neruda, 'Poetry' translated by Alastair Reid, Souvenir Press.

From The Epic of Gilgamesh, Translated with an Introduction by N. K. Sandars published by Penguin Press. Copyright © N. K. Sandars, 1973. Reprinted by permission of Penguin Books Limited.

William Stafford, "The Way It Is" from Ask Me: 100 Essential Poems. Copyright © 1998 by William Stafford and the Estate of William Stafford. Reprinted with the permission of The Permissions Company, LLC on behalf of Kim Stafford and Graywolf Press, Minneapolis, Minnesota, www.graywolfpress.org.

Excerpt from WITHOUT END: NEW AND SELECTED POEMS by Adam Zagajewski; Translated by Clare Cavanagh and Renata Gorczynski, Benjamin Ivry, and C. K. Williams. Copyright © 2002 by Adam Zagajewski. 2 Translation copyright © 2002 by Farrar, Straus and Giroux. Reprinted by permission of Farrar, Straus and Giroux. All Rights Reserved.

Batsford is committed to respecting the intellectual property rights of others. We have taken all reasonable efforts to ensure that the reproduction of all contents on these pages is done with the full consent of the copyright owners. If you are aware of unintentional omissions, please contact the company directly so that any necessary corrections may be made for future editions.

ACKNOWLEDGEMENTS

A very big thank you to the great team at Batsford for their continued support, particularly to my editor Rebecca Armstrong. It was a pleasure to work with Rebecca on this book. My thanks also go to all the poets featured in this book who might not have predicted that their poems would help tell the story of the poetry of the Zodiac.

ABOUT THE EDITOR

Liz Ison studied English Literature at the University of Cambridge. Since 2015, Liz has been leading shared reading groups in person and online as well as workshops encouraging people to enjoy and rediscover poetry. Her anthologies include *100 Poems to Help You Heal, 100 Poems to Help You Relax, 100 Poems to Grow Your Confidence, A Poem to Read Aloud Every Day of the Year* and *A Literary Letter for Every Day of the Year*. Liz's star sign is Libra. She lives in London.

First published in the United Kingdom
in 2026 by
Batsford
43 Great Ormond Street
London
WC1N 3HZ

An imprint of B. T. Batsford Holdings Limited

Copyright © B. T. Batsford Ltd 2026

All rights reserved. No part of this publication may be copied, displayed, extracted, reproduced, utilized, stored in a retrieval system or transmitted in any form or by any means, electronic, mechanical or otherwise including but not limited to photocopying, recording, or scanning without the prior written permission of the publishers.

ISBN 9781837330430

A CIP catalogue record for this book is available from the British Library.

10 9 8 7 6 5 4 3 2 1

Reproduction by Mission Productions, Hong Kong
Printed by Dream Colour, China

This book can be ordered direct from the publisher at
www.batsfordbooks.com, or try your local bookshop.

Distributed throughout the UK and Europe by Abrams & Chronicle Books, 1st Floor, 22–24 Ely Place, London EC1N 6TE and 57 rue Gaston Tessier, 75166 Paris, France

www.abramsandchronicle.co.uk
info@abramsandchronicle.co.uk